Contents

Start creating the fireplace of your dreams here.

Are you looking for innovative ways to incorporate a fireplace into a home you currently own or one you are planning to buy or build? Does your existing fireplace simply need a fresh new face? Or does a complete overhaul come to mind? You've no doubt answered yes to one of these questions, and you've come to the right place.

Every page of this book brims with decorating and design ideas that can help you make any fireplace both as practical and as beautiful as possible. For your convenience, the book has been divided into five photo-intensive chapters.

Chapter 1, Reflections of Style, includes dozens of inspirational photographs that portray the most popular hearth decorating styles, such as traditional, Old World, American country, Arts and Crafts, contemporary, and eclectic. Within these pages, you'll also find hearths adorned with an array of surfacing options that blend seamlessly with the surrounding decor; others underscore decorative focal points that set the design tone for a room.

Chapter 2, Room by Room, provides a photographic journal of fireplaces found in every room of the home, including living rooms, family rooms, great-rooms, libraries, dining rooms, kitchens, bedrooms, baths, connecting rooms, lower levels, and outdoor living spaces. Tips on maximizing space to make room for a fireplace as well as how to balance this element with other elements, such as the television, are also included.

Chapter 3, Alternative Options, takes an in-depth look at all the fuel sources for fireplaces on the market including wood-burning options, gas-burning models, freestanding stoves, and other alternatives available for both indoor and outdoor use. This chapter takes the guesswork out of choosing the right fireplace for your room setting and budget. You'll get a good understanding of how these various appliances work, and get answers to important questions: Just what is a direct-vent fireplace? Is it possible to have a fireplace without a vent? How well do the various models heat a room? Are there air-quality issues with any configurations? Information on how you can create the look and feel of a fireplace with candelabras, and other attractive kinetic lighting solutions that require little remodeling effort will also be included.

Chapter 4, Decorating a Fireplace, is where you'll find inspiration and advice for decorating the spaces around a fireplace, for example, the hearth, the mantel, and the mantelshelf. This chapter also expands on surfacing options for the hearth introduced in Chapter 1, the surround, and the mantel featuring before and after photos of some extreme hearth makeovers.

Chapter 5, Fireplace Know-How, provides advice on how to inspect, clean, and maintain your fireplace to better ensure years of fail-safe operation. Step-by-step photos illustrate how to install a direct-vent gas fireplace. Guidance on choosing firewood and building a fire in a wood-burning model is also included.

Better Homes and Gardens®

fireplace

design & decorating ideas

Meredith® Books
Des Moines, Iowa

Better Homes and Gardens® *Fireplace Design & Decorating Ideas*
Editor: Paula Marshall
Project Manager: Amber Barz
Contributing Editors: Katie Anderson, Cathy Long
Graphic Designer: David Jordan
Copy Chief: Terri Fredrickson
Publishing Operations Manager: Karen Schirm
Senior Editor, Asset and Information Manager: Phillip Morgan
Edit and Design Production Coordinator: Mary Lee Gavin
Editorial Assistant: Kaye Chabot
Book Production Managers: Pam Kvitne, Marjorie J. Schenkelberg, Rick von Holdt, Mark Weaver
Contributing Copy Editor: Ira Lacher
Contributing Proofreaders: Kristin Bienert, Tom Blackett, Becky Danley, Ann Marie Sapienza
Cover Photographer: Michael Partenio
Indexer: Kathleen Poole

Meredith® **Books**
Executive Director, Editorial: Gregory H. Kayko
Executive Director, Design: Matt Strelecki
Executive Editor/Group Manager: Denise Caringer
Marketing Product Manager: Tyler Woods

Publisher and Editor in Chief: James D. Blume
Editorial Director: Linda Raglan Cunningham
Executive Director, New Business Development: Todd M. Davis
Executive Director, Sales: Ken Zagor
Director, Operations: George A. Susral
Director, Production: Douglas M. Johnston
Director, Marketing: Amy Nichols
Business Director: Jim Leonard

Vice President and General Manager: Douglas J. Guendel

Better Homes and Gardens® **Magazine**
Editor in Chief: Karol DeWulf Nickell
Deputy Editor, Home Design: Oma Blaise Ford

Meredith Publishing Group
President: Jack Griffin
Executive Vice President: Bob Mate

Meredith Corporation
Chairman and Chief Executive Officer: William T. Kerr
President and Chief Operating Officer: Stephen M. Lacy

In Memoriam: E.T. Meredith III (1933-2003)

All of us at Meredith® Books are dedicated to providing you with information and ideas to enhance your home. We welcome your comments and suggestions. Write to us at: Meredith Books, Home Decorating and Design Editorial Department, 1716 Locust St., Des Moines, IA 50309-3023.

If you would like to purchase any of our home decorating and design, cooking, crafts, gardening, or home improvement books, check wherever quality books are sold. Or visit us at: bhgbooks.com

Chapter 1

Reflections of Style

From the elaborately carved hearths adorning the interiors of sprawling French Chateaux to the mortar-and-stone surrounds found in woodland cabins, dancing flames are a captivating central feature of homes throughout the world. In this chapter, each featured fireplace highlights a different decorating style including traditional, Old World, American country, Arts and Crafts, contemporary, and eclectic. As you consider the right fireplace style for your home, trust your instincts. Surround your fireplace with colors that cheer you, fabrics that comfort you, and treasures that capture your past and your future.

Carved stone surrounds warmed European castles as far back as the Middle Ages.

Old World

In the stately homes of 17th-century Europe, grand stone hearths provided welcome warmth and an enticing gathering spot for family. To re-create this Old-World fireside look in your own home, think big. In this time-proven style, hearths, mantels, and surrounds are all weighty in appearance and large compared with other fireplace styles.

Check with architectural salvage firms for antique stone or marble fireplace surrounds, or look into cast-stone versions that mimic these more expensive materials. In the great room, *left*, a stucco surround replicates the look of a solid stone hearth. In the living room featured on pages 10-11, the stone-look surround was cast on the spot in concrete, then glazed to look centuries old. Floors of natural or simulated stone, slate, or large-scale tiles complement this vintage fireplace style well, as does salvaged wood flooring. Give walls more visual weight by topping them

This large-scale fireplace is made from stucco and blends in with the adjoining wall finish used throughout the great room. A large-square terra-cotta tile floor complements the Old-World design theme.

with elaborate moldings and glazing them to replicate vintage plaster.

When choosing fireplace screens and tools, opt for the hefty look of wrought iron, pewter, or antique brass. For furnishings, select deep, generously sized upholstered pieces and sturdy tables that are proportional to the scale of the fireplace. These substantial pieces keep the weight of the room visually balanced.

The Right Light

Illuminate your fireplace with the right fixtures and it will stay stylishly aglow even without a fire.

To light a picture over the mantel, use a recessed, adjustable "eyeball" fixture mounted in the ceiling, about 3 feet out from the fireplace wall. To highlight the hearth and surround, install a recessed downlight or surface-mounted accent light on the ceiling about 18 inches from the fireplace wall.

Installing a pair of wall sconces? Locate them no more than 6 inches in from the outer edges of the mantel and at least 12 inches above the mantelshelf as shown here.

LEFT: Replicating a centuries-old stone model, this concrete fireplace creates an Old-World look in a new living room. Glazing the concrete with a translucent dye creates the illusion of age. Vintage accessories and antique brass tools add a touch of elegance.

Romantic

Free-flowing interpretations of romantic style combine motifs from ancient Rome, Greece, France, and Egypt to achieve a sumptuous and glamorous look of gilded finishes and ornate detailing. To bring this classic look to your home, choose a formal fireplace that combines refined materials such as marble and hand-carved wood or stone with graceful proportions, as shown *below*. Center an ornate mirror or an oil painting over the fireplace, and dress the mantel with a symmetrical arrangement of classic objects, such as vases and candlesticks. Surround your focal-point fireplace with sofas, chairs, and longues with scrolled arms and backs. Favored fabrics include lustrous silks, sumptuous damasks, and tactile velvets and chenilles. Warm whites and buttery finishes are staples, but rich golds and deep burgundies are often added to warm the room.

RIGHT: **Give a plain fireplace surround a romantic look with a decorative painting treatment. In this room both the fireplace and walls are finished with hand-troweled texturing in a scroll-like pattern that resembles aged, faded plaster.**

BELOW: **A custom mantel and surround of statuary marble grace this Victorian-style fireplace. Elaborately carved wood moldings enhance the room's romantic look.**

Bring a touch of romance to your fireplace surround by topping the mantel with vintage vases, fresh flowers, and a still-life oil painting.

A marble mantelpiece and elaborate carvings distinguish this salvaged surround.

The White Way An all-white room provides a perfect starting point for romantic style. Warm the cool palette with layers of linens in warm white tones, an array of vintage accessories that sparkle and shine, and as much textural variation as possible.

For the fireplace choose a surround that is intricately detailed with elaborate moldings, delicate carvings, or hand-painted designs.

ABOVE: A combination of black granite and richly stained woods make the fireplace a focal point of this family room.

RIGHT: Fluted columns and a honed marble surround accompany the traditional styling of this somewhat formal living room. Arch-top display shelves fill the flanking walls.

Traditional

Meticulously designed, traditional style fireplaces such as the ones featured here never go out of style. Symmetrical arrangements of cabinetry and fixtures create a feeling of balance and order. Architectural details include deep crown moldings, customary chair rails, finely crafted woodwork, and lustrous stained and painted surfaces. A pleasing combination of gentle curves and rectilinear shapes are also part of the look often created by combining rounded columns with geometric cabinetry panels. Colors frequently are in the mid-range of tones, though very dark and very light hues can also be used to accent. Fabrics typically are made from high-quality natural materials, such as fine silks, heavy linens, and rich wools in classic patterns that include florals, botanicals, checks, plaids, tone-on-tone stripes, and solids. Natural surfaces that complement a traditional hearth and include marble, granite, or limestone surrounds and wood plank or stone tile floors. Vintage accessories including shiny metal hardware, sconces, urns, framed prints, hand-painted ceramics, and cut glass bottles and vases. In the living room *above left,* handcrafted cherry cabinets frame the hearth and combine with painted woodwork and traditional columns to create a classic look.

ABOVE: The original brick facade on this fireplace had become rather tired and dated looking. As part of a complete room redo, honed limestone was installed around the fireplace and a full suite of crisp white molding gives the room a relaxed classic look.

Country

Snug and simply furnished, the ranches and farmhouses that sheltered generations of rural Americans have left a legacy of comfortable style that is as well-suited to urban high rises and suburban ranches as it is to log cabins and clapboard colonials.

Whether you're looking for a casual or a refined country look, keep the millwork simple: A shallow mantel adorned with simple accessories creates an understated background. For an even more authentic Early American look, install a vintage painted mantel over a firebox made from salvaged bricks, as shown *opposite*, or cover the mantel wall with paneling evoking images of Early American homes as *below*. Add classical elements, such as the keystone at the peak of the arch, *below*, or the fluted pilasters flanking the surround, *opposite*, for a more formal hearth.

Country-style interiors are natural showcases for heirlooms and

OPPOSITE: Wearing worn blue paint, this salvaged fireplace mantel serves as the focal point of a country dining room. Tall finials, paintings of various sizes, a child's chair, and a few fireplace accessories turn the simple arrangement into a country still life.

BELOW: An Early American color scheme gives this fireplace surround a vintage look. Colors from the polished marble surround repeat in the upholstery fabrics on the side chairs and on the toss pillows.

Country style can be rustic or refined, but it always invites people to gather at the hearth.

collectibles. Pedigreed quilts and priceless pottery will look right at home, but don't hesitate to incorporate sentimental favorites. Americana decor in the colors of the flag are a perfect complement to a country home adorned with pine-clad walls and Douglas fir floors. To create a warm, instant gathering spot, drape a well-worn quilt over a fireside table or a granny-square afghan across the back of the sofa.

Beaded-board walls and ceilings evoke images of porches and kitchens past, setting an informal tone. Millwork in casual country is often stockier with fewer "refining" features, and fireplace surrounds are sometimes of rough masonry to give the look of having been "harvested" from nearby fields.

LEFT: Granite blocks arranged in dry-stack style create this rustic fireplace surround.

BELOW: This knotty-pine-clad fireplace blends in with the walls. To reduce the amount of space the fireplace takes up, it's built into a corner, and the shelves recessed in an arched niche above the mantel add display space.

Cottage

The appealing mix of comfort, simplicity, and nostalgia that characterizes American country style also marks the interiors of many cottages lining the beaches of America's waters. The lines of cottage design are softer than country; the furnishings rounder. Create this welcoming look by arranging faded chintz upholstered pieces and slipcovered furnishings in front of a mantel covered with hand-painted chinaware, garden-grown flowers, or seaside treasures. Cover the walls with pale shades often associated with summers at the beach—ocean blue or green, sky blue, sandy beige, or sea-glass green. Baskets of seashells or artwork depicting beach scenes, seashells, or botanical prints perfectly accent the hearth. Mimic the softer look in the hearth by using smooth finishes or curvy lines that reflect the softer side of natural. The mantra of cottage is comfort and ease; the mantel and surround of a cottage-style hearth should convey the same breezy attitude.

RIGHT: Scrolls and seashell shapes on this vintage surround add a romantic touch to a cottage-style gathering space.

BELOW: A large-scale fireplace is less intrusive recessed into a beaded-board sidewall. The mantelshelf and accessories finished in the same creamy tones as the wall keep the focus on the artwork above the mantel.

Solid oak woodwork and strong rectilinear elements are staples of Arts and Crafts style.

Arts and Crafts

At the turn of the 20th century, whole neighborhoods of snug bungalows with built-in bookcases, benches, and buffets sprang up furnished with the solid, austere oak furniture dubbed Craftsman- or Mission-style.

Give your fireside an Arts and Crafts appeal using a palette of cream, terra-cotta, earthy brown, and sage green. Keep the mantel and hearth design boldly simple, with square corners and a few sturdy flourishes. Tile and brick facades with plank wood mantels create the desired geometric design and solid feel.

Choose furniture pieces with no-nonsense lines covered in sturdy fabrics with subtle patterns in rich, earthy colors; leather is a good choice too. Cover windows with muslin or linen panels. Landscape paintings, matte-finish pottery, and lamps with hammered copper-color bases and glass shades are ideal accents. Warm wood floors with woven area rugs feature a simple handwoven design.

OPPOSITE: A geometric tile pattern gives this fireplace surround an updated Arts and Crafts look. The simply designed mantel features the solid woodwork used throughout the house.

BELOW: A flip of a switch lights this energy-efficient gas fireplace. The upper portion of the bump-out required to create the fireplace holds a television set. (Two matching panels slip from the sides to hide the television when it's not in use.) The rounded lines of the upholstered pieces give the room a softened, blended country/Mission-style look.

A frame of posts and beams defining the fireplace setting is another signature Arts and Crafts detail.

BELOW: This gas fireplace warms what was once an unfinished basement. Built-ins flanking the fireplace are fitted with old-fashioned reeded glass doors. Corner posts give the space the look of an inglenook.

RIGHT: This fireplace alcove gives the entire room a cozy, intimate feel. The earthy colors in the tiled surround provided the color cues used throughout the house. Slim dark wood accents give the space a light look.

Lodge

About the time America tamed its wilderness, nostalgia for the wild set in. As Mission-style cottages were being built along city streets, rustic camps and vacation lodges started springing up across the country from the Adirondacks to Yellowstone National Park. The wealthy might forgo big-city comforts to rough it without electricity or running water, but the comforting essential heart of every wilderness home was its massive and welcoming stone fireplace.

Today a fireplace of rugged unpolished granite or fieldstone worn smooth by centuries exposed to the elements still suggests the snug comfort and relaxed ways of vacation hideaways. Beamed ceilings and wood plank floors are natural companions to rough-cut fireplace surfaces. Rag rugs and wicker or twig chairs add further natural textures, and a collection of handwoven baskets or bowls brings a touch of the outdoors to the inside. Another popular choice is to use accents and patterns with natural motifs, such as leaves, outlines of trees, animal silhouettes, or branches. Deep natural colors—pine green and deep-water blue—add a richness to lodge-style rooms.

Though exposed chimneys and open rafters are more familiar elements of lodge-style interiors, the room *above* presents a rather genteel variation with its honed-stone tile surround and raised hearth. The contrast of rough and smooth, light and dark, gives the room a cheerful, inviting air. The great room in the lodge, *opposite,* features a barrel-vaulted ceiling and a rustic native stone surround.

ABOVE: **This lodge-look fireplace features a 50-year-old walnut mantelpiece and a raised hearth that offers seating for guests. The raised hearth also puts the enchanting flames at eye level for everyone sitting in the room.**

OPPOSITE: **A stone hearth, curved beams, and unadorned windows combine for a strong design statement in this lodge-style home. Simple furnishings with touches of bright, regional colors enhance the natural materials that warm the area.**

Cape Cod

Though more refined than the lodge look, Cape Cod-style hearths and homes also welcome casual living and nature-inspired beauty. Indigenous material, from smooth woods and heavily textured stones to earthy colors, invite guests and family members to come in and relax.

Consider choosing cherry, maple, or mahogany cabinets stained a pale honey or rustic red tone. When combined with a warm-color stain, the fine graining in these woods brings coziness to a hearth area without overpowering the other decorative elements. As shown *right,* rough-hewn limestones are the perfect choice for this Cape Cod style surround.

If you plan to extend the stone fireplace facade clear to the ceiling, as shown *opposite,* consider using cultured stone; this man-made material is much lighter in weight and easier to install than natural stone.

As with other nature-inspired motifs Cape Cod-style homes are best decorated with soothing colors from nature including sage greens, clay reds, and warm wood tones. Underscore views and sunlight with large picture windows

and French doors adorned with unfussy, straightforward window coverings such as Roman shades or sheer panels.

ABOVE: **Made from stacked limestone, the fireplace serves as a focal point in this eclectically decorated living room. The hefty mantel is a good counterpoint to the heavy** stone surround and provides ample display space for an array of items.

OPPOSITE: **Cultured river rock runs top to bottom, accenting the height of the vaulted ceiling. Divided light windows flank the fireplace, providing a generous view of the woodland setting beyond.**

LEFT: Made from cultured stone, a floor-to-ceiling fireplace like this looks real but can be installed without reinforcing floor joists. It's sufficiently visually interesting to need very little additional adornment.

BELOW: This natural limestone fireplace surround and hearth directed the color choices for the room. That choice means the character of a relatively small hearth fills the large room.

Southwest

The architecture of the American Southwest has its own vocabulary—literally and figuratively. Exteriors are fashioned of adobe—a mix of clay, sand, and straw—which can be made into blocks or applied like stucco.

The kiva, a distinctive beehive-shape fireplace, *below,* echoes the ceremonial chambers of the region's ancient Native Americans. Smooth and gently rounded, kivas are built with shallow, angled walls that radiate heat outward more efficiently than many conventional fireplace designs.

You can bring Southwest style to your fireside, even if it's not a kiva. Depending on your tastes, choose a menu of earth-inspired colors anchored by saturated tones of bold teal and coral or sun-bleached shades of terra-cotta and turquoise. Leather-covered sofas and chairs lend an authentic Southwestern flavor, especially when they're topped with throws or coverlets reminiscent of traditional trading blankets. Rustic wood chairs, tables, and cupboards of pine or aspen recall the region's early furnishings. The designs are practical with little adornment.

Consider covering the fireplace surround with brightly glazed Mexican tiles or installing an earth-tone floor of oversize matte-finish tiles. Add pottery, baskets, and nubby woven rugs that incorporate time-honored Native American symbols such as stylized deer, birds, and fish. True Southwest architecture features heavy structural ceiling beams called vigas; add nonfunctional rough-hewn log beams for the same effect.

LEFT: The mass and materials of this outdoor hearth complement the home's Southwestern design even though the basic components, the firebox and flue, are the same used in most modern fireplaces. The mantel is fashioned from a salvaged cypress beam, adding to the effect.

BELOW: This beehive-shaped fireplace, called a kiva, is placed in the corner, a popular choice for this style. It's such a distinctive choice that the room's decor most often reflects the same Southwestern sensibility.

Eclectic

"If you like it, you can make it work," is the mantra of this popular design style. The term "eclectic" was first used to describe bungalows reflecting a jumble of styles—Spanish Colonial, English Tudor, and French Chateau—that often included arched doorways, plain cabinetry, carved columns, and fireplaces slathered in decorative plaster. The fireplace *left* typifies the appealing, but hard-to-categorize, fireplaces in many such homes.

If your fireplace seems out of sync with your decorating style, coax it into compliance. On page 38, the modern shape of the white upholstered chairs complements the white frame of the squared-off windows. Rustic stacked stone surround provides unexpected texture as well as a visual connection to the woodland scene outside the windows. A row of small, complementary prints on the mantel adds color without detracting from the rest of the scene.

Color also offers an easy and excellent way to visually connect unrelated items, as shown in the gathering room on page 39. Neutral tones visually link a classic fireplace surround and traditional architectural elements with contemporary furnishings and a variety of accessories.

LEFT: **This concrete-look mantel and hearth are actually wood-frame structures fitted with wire mesh and covered with hand-troweled mortar and plaster. The gray tones radiate outward through the room in the coffee table and console table.**

Mixing and matching architecture, furnishings, and fixtures from different periods results in an eclectic-style room.

BELOW: A direct-vent fireplace was a necessity as there is no place to run a conventional chimney. The fireplace and surrounding view are the first things guests see when they come through the home's front door. The unusual combination of windows and stone make a memorable design statement.

RIGHT: The mix of styles in this living room makes the space neither overly formal nor too casual, a perfect compromise for a couple with two very different decorating styles.

Contemporary

If you consider yourself more new wave than old world, opt for a fireplace with clean lines and subtle contours that will repeat in the room's decor. Create this cosmopolitan look by paring your room down. Bare floors, minimal window treatments, and exposed construction elements such as ceiling trusses or fireplace flues set the stage. Look for clean-lined furnishings that mix modern industrial materials with natural textures such as leather and linen along with natural look-alikes such as animal- and botanical-print fabrics.

Choose sofas and chairs with exposed legs rather than skirted styles; then add a splash of glass with a coffee table that reflects its stylish surroundings. Consider flat-front cabinets in a light, subtly grained wood such as ash, birch, or maple, or with solid-color laminate fronts, or opt for a flat, natural tile surround. For extra shine, choose a shiny black granite surround and a curved glass fire screen, as shown on page 42. In the living area *left*, smooth expanses of limestone and sleek cherry wood cabinets visually enlarge the small space.

LEFT: Stone slabs and flat-front cabinetry give this fireplace a sleek, modern look. Three metal statues displayed on the small, rounded mantelshelf add a touch of whimsy.

Inviting Contemporary The key to bringing warmth and charm to a contemporary-style room is to choose colors and materials that are warm and welcoming as they are clean-lined.

Natural or lightly stained honey-tone and red woods bring instant warmth into a room, as do soft fabrics such as satin, silk, and faux suede, as well as warm colors such as pumpkin, red, and yellow.

Soften crisp edges by tossing in a few curves, such as a coffee table with a round glass top or a mantelshelf in the shape of a half-moon.

ABOVE: Black granite tiles accentuate this simple fireplace surround. The rounded glass fire screen mimics the curves of the side tables and mirrors and gives the fireplace a distinctive modern twist.

RIGHT: The white painted square of molding above this mantel visually extends the art display space, drawing the eye down from the vaulted ceiling. Stacked windows flanking the fireplace surround bring in light and balance the display niches and shelves.

Clean lines mix with soft curves in these contemporary-style rooms.

Personal Best

Personal style makes your hearth area sing its own special song. Whether the lyrics you choose are romantic, jazzy, moody, or something in between, your passions and penchants are expressed in this one-of-a-kind design scheme. If you prefer a mantel that looks like none

BELOW: The simple design of the fireplace's solid-surfacing surround and a floating wood mantel creates a personal look that's a cross between traditional and contemporary. This choice also saved the owners of this home a lot of money in construction and material costs.

A tumbled-marble surround, raised curved hearth, and recessed display niche above the hearth make the fireplace in this master suite a one-of-a-kind focal point. Imagine how plain the space would look if the fireplace wall were flat and square.

other, draw a sketch of what you have in mind and take it to a design professional to have construction drawings made. Whether you're looking for an amiable melding of styles from opposite sides of the Atlantic or a soaring fire space to fill an entire wall, with a little imagination and a lot of heart you can make it happen.

Part of a brand-new Greek Revival home, this unusual fireplace appears centuries old thanks to a painted brick facade and a distressed wood mantel.

Painted Beauty One of the easiest and most affordable ways to update a fireplace is with paint. Although these white-painted bricks are new, you can make old, soot-stained bricks look equally as attractive by scrubbing them down and adding a few coats of paint. To view a mantel that has been updated with paint, turn to page 143.

ABOVE: Modern fireplace styles have sleek lines and smooth surfaces, but the most pleasing hearths still have echoes of the fireplace's traditional styling. Note the streamlined classic mantel here. The polished stone hearth reflects the fire's energetic flames.

UPPER RIGHT: The rustic setting of this room is well-suited to the traditional deep brick firebox of this hearth. The generous size of this fireplace reflects its practical history.

RIGHT: The joy of modern engineering means you can have any mantel style with all the conveniences, such as this two-sided gas fireplace wrapped with an elaborate surround.

A spark in time

Fireplaces have always been important stylistically, setting the tone for everything else in a room. If you're renovating an older home—or just hoping to make a new house feel old—you might want to do a little research on which styles were prevalent during your favorite period. Here's a quick rundown of fireplace fashions from the past few centuries.

Tudor and Jacobean. During the Tudor and Jacobean periods in Britain, hearths were grandly scaled with broad lintels spanning cavernous openings. Mantelpiece designs were as elaborate as any you might find in a church.

1500–1625

Neoclassic. During the late 1700s and early 1800s, designers looked to Greece and Rome. Wooden surrounds and overmantels featured a great deal of finery. Homeowners who could afford a solid marble surround often embraced simpler designs with less ornamentation. Others settled for marble slips and gussied up the woodwork.

1795–1850

Arts and Crafts. Arts and Crafts fireplaces featured clean, simple lines and spare geometry. But not everything was rectilinear. Sinewy vines, stylized leaves and flowers, elegant long-tailed birds—all appeared during the Arts and Crafts era, in art-tile accents, as well as mantels made of beaten copper and cast iron.

1860–1920

Art Deco. One thing can always be said about Art Deco: It made waves! Popular motifs, such as wavy borders and "stepping" patterns, made their way into fireplace designs during this period.

1910–1940

1600–1775

1715–1840

Georgian. During the early Georgian period (the early 1700s), fashionable Europeans ordered elaborately carved mantels and paired them with marble slips. Classical designs—wave patterns, scrolling acanthus leaves, Ionic pilasters at the sides—gave mantels added grace.

Colonial American. In early colonial America, it was common to forgo the overmantel and hang a large painting above the fireplace. Wall paneling often surrounded the entire fireplace, framing it like a showpiece.

1830–1905

Victorian. Victorians had no fear of ornamentation, either—though their fireplace designs frequently took a more Gothic turn and embraced medieval European traditions. Built-in cabinetry, raised paneling, elaborate overmantels with spindles and fretwork—any or all of these might be gathered around the hearth to underscore its importance.

1920–1960

1950–1970

American Modernism. The operative word for American Modernism is sleek. Look for long, lean lines with few adornments. Some fireplaces in this style don't even have mantels.

Prairie Style. Frank Lloyd Wright, the prominent architect when this style first appeared, often included a central fireplace, dividing rooms in what was then a daringly open plan. Plainspoken natural materials add to the earthy quality of these homes.

Chapter 2

Room by Room

Before central heating, a bedroom fireplace was a necessity, staving off winter's chill. Now bedroom fireplaces offer a touch of luxury and romance. They are equally as enticing when installed in a master bath. Remodeling your basement? Give it a warm glow with a fireplace. On your patio, a fireplace is the perfect companion for watching the sunset or gazing at the stars.

Gathering Rooms

A fireplace immediately adds comfort and character to any room, and it cues family and friends to the room's personality. A stately, formal fireplace sets the living room apart as a spot for special occasions. In the family room or great room a casual fireplace of rustic stone signals everyone to relax and unwind. Light a fire in the dining room or kitchen fireplace and without speaking a word, you've invited guests to linger long after the table is cleared.

Before central heating, a bedroom fireplace was a necessity to keep the room warm during winter. Now bedroom fireplaces offer a touch of luxury and romance. They are equally as inviting when installed in a master bath.

Remodeling your basement? Give it a warm glow and sense of coziness with a fireplace. On your patio or sunroom a fireplace is the perfect enhancement for drinking a cup of your favorite morning brew or evening bubbly.

To get the most satisfaction from all of your fire-lit days and evenings, plan the details within the context of individual rooms.

A wide tile surround and a large painting above the mantel make this living room fireplace a focal point of the seating area.

The inviting glow of a fireplace adds a sense of welcome to any gathering room.

Living Room

Living rooms, family rooms, and great-rooms are the most popular spaces for fireplaces. These gathering areas are designed for entertaining and family togetherness. A glowing fire only adds to the room's warmth and welcome.

When selecting the appropriate space for a hearth in any of these gathering spaces, consider the room's views, media equipment, and traffic pattern. If the room has nice views, orient the fireplace 90 degrees from the best vista so that the furniture arrangement takes advantage of both focal points. If the view is less than desir-able, make the fireplace the central focal point of the room by centering it on the window wall and covering the remaining windows with sheer window treatments, or stained or frosted glass.

In any living space, set off the mantel and surround by finishing it in a color that contrasts with the walls. Draw more attention to the mantel by topping it with oversize artwork. Custom-made doors or a hand-forged wrought-iron screen will draw attention to the firebox. To create extra guest seating and to give the hearth more prominence, raise it 12 to 18 inches above the floor, and be sure the depth is at least 12 inches.

Encourage guests to gather in front of the fire by grouping chairs, sofas, or love seats close to the fireplace and defining the gathering spot with an area rug. Be sure to include end tables, or a coffee table, within easy reach of all the seating pieces. Leave ample space between the fireplace opening and the furnishings for easy access and comfort as well as safety.

If the room also contains media equipment such as a television or stereo, consider adding custom cabinetry around the fireplace to accommodate the equipment. Or move the fireplace to the corner of a room to provide more wall space for built-ins.

Avoid placing a fireplace between doors or next to a hallway that makes it difficult to gather by the fire without impeding traffic flow. If you choose to turn attention away from your fireplace, neutralize it by painting it the same color as the surrounding walls, facing seating pieces away from it rather than toward it, and leaving the mantel clear of any accessories.

OPPOSITE: **Raising the height of this small Swedish-style fireplace places the flames at eye level for guests seated in the overstuffed fireside chairs. A 6-foot-tall tile surround and a niche adorned with a painted mural make the fireplace a prominent feature of the room.**

LEFT: **A cast-concrete fireplace surrounded by recessed shelving makes this living room fireplace a focal point.**

Family Room

activities, keep fireside seating comfortable and casual. Choose relaxed, deep-cushioned chairs and sofas with rounded arms and backs to accommodate sprawling teenagers and the occasional afternoon nap for Mom or Dad. Avoid delicate brocades and pale silks. Turn to tough fabrics such as leather, denim, or nubby tweeds. If you prefer light colors, select washable cottons, cotton blends, and man-made fibers with subtle overall patterns that disguise dirt. For even less upkeep, treat all family room fabrics and area rugs to repel stains and spills.

Add even more comfort with a generous stack of accent pillows and warm and washable afghans, blankets, or throws. Consider keeping a big basket piled with sturdy oversize pillows. Have them nearby, ready to be pulled out for extra floor seating around a coffee table or up close to a crackling fire. Slipcover the pillows in washable fabric that coordinates with the color scheme of the room.

At the same time you add your fireplace, build in needed storage for books and games. Combine high shelves for displaying treasures, medium-height shelves for easy access, and closed cabinets that hide clutter.

Whether a sleek, contemporary surround is your preference, perhaps a rugged fieldstone model, or even a traditional white Colonial Williamsburg surround, fireplaces provide perfect gathering spots for everyday family togetherness, from the bedlam of board game battles to the snuggly quiet of bedtime story reading. To make your fireplace more welcoming for family

If you prefer to keep the television out of sight when it's not in use, consider hiding it behind a painting that slides out of the way for viewing.

LEFT: This framed Caribbean watercolor slides up and down via a motorized track that is operated by remote control, keeping the television completely out of sight when not in use. For a less high-tech alternative, attach hinges on one side of the picture to swing the picture to the side for TV viewing.

ABOVE: Locating a fireplace in the corner of the room frees up wall space for other furnishings. This Southwestern-style fireplace tucks between patio doors and an entertainment hutch. An L-shape sofa combines with an easy chair to keep both television and fireplace in direct view.

Great Room

A grand room calls for a grand fireplace. Ensure that the model you choose creates an adequate presence. In this spacious room adding an overmantel, as shown *below,* and a raised hearth were good choices. Make a small fireplace opening seem larger by increasing the size of the tile or stone surround and by adding a large mantel. Choose furnishings that complement the room size: Surround a large fireplace in a large-scale room with oversized, overstuffed upholstered pieces. Then anchor the arrangement with a colorful, patterned area rug.

A change in ceiling height or flooring materials defines activity areas within a great room, as do partial walls or perimeter pillars. Arrange the furniture in each area so that the fireplace can be seen from each area, and that one area focuses on the hearth.

OPPOSITE: **Concrete stones and glass windowpanes combine to create a stunning backdrop for this contemporary wood-burning fireplace. The exposed steel chimney adds an industrial look.**

BELOW: **The limestone that fronts this house was also used on the great room fireplace surround. The generous scale of the entire hearth complements the size of the room.**

Make the great room feel more cozy and inviting with a large-scale fireplace that can be seen from every activity area.

The green veining in the marble surround of this fireplace plays up the Victorian-era wall color. Raising the firebox two feet above the floor gives everyone in the room—even from across the room—a clear view of the fire.

Space Misers Built-ins on either side of a fireplace can lend a serene note of architectural symmetry to an office or den while providing practical storage for office supplies. Adding a bench to one side or the other expands seating options for guests or four-footed friends.

Library

Whether you call it a home office, a den, or a library, these intimate rooms are evermore inviting when warmed by a fire. Imagine getting up in the morning, slipping on a robe, and heading to "work" in a room lit by flickering flames and the rising sun. For best fireside viewing when seated at a desk, raise the hearth a minimum of one foot above the floor.

On the evening of an all-too-hectic day, head back to the cozy room with a cup of warm tea and a good book, and let the kids take over the family room. If space is precious, install a corner fireplace similar to the one featured on page 59 or squeeze a direct-vent unit between a pair of narrow windows. By making this quiet working room as inviting as possible, you'll increase your productivity whether you work from home on a daily basis or only when you have to pay the bills.

A marble hearth and surround combine with a cherry mantel and floor-to-ceiling paneling to create a cozy atmosphere in this spacious den. Leather furnishings lend a masculine air.

Dining Room

A fireplace in the dining room encourages guests and family members to relax and linger long after the dishes are cleared. Depending on the proportions of your eating area, you can place the table at a right angle to the fireplace or parallel to it.

Keep comfort in mind: If you seat diners too close to the fire, the heat may be overwhelming. If the temperature is too warm in the house to light a

log or gas fire, fill the hearth with pillar candles and create a candlelit glow without the heat.

ABOVE: **Open to the kitchen, this hearth-warmed eating area doubles as a family play space and reading center.**

OPPOSITE: **Although brand-new, this wood-burning fireplace with a rough-brick surround looks as if it might have been built during Colonial times.**

Dining by firelight encourages family and friends to linger long after the plates are cleared.

To create a personal decorating statement in your dining room, dress the fireplace mantel with favorite objects and artwork that are inviting. Paintings depicting fruits, flowers, wines, and patisseries are traditional dining area favorites, as are vintage plates. Shine your prized crystal and set out candlesticks and other cherished pieces of polished brass, silver, and copper. They'll gleam even brighter in the glow of a fire.

RIGHT: In this dining room, a custom-made firescreen complements the geometric patterns on the built-in china cabinets and on the inset just below the mantel.

BELOW: A direct-vent gas fireplace encourages the family to gather and linger in this dining area every morning and night. A window above the fireplace brings in natural light and views.

Kitchen

Once upon a time, every kitchen had a fireplace. From the thatched cottages of England to the log cabins of America's pioneers, the kitchen was often a part of a single large room where most daily activities took place. Drawing close to the hearth's warmth and brightness, rural families prepared and ate their meals, shared stories, and welcomed friends to gather by the hearth. Fireplace openings were large enough to cook a week's worth of bread and a full side of beef.

You may not aspire to something quite that ambitious. But if you like the idea of old-fashioned, open-fire cooking and choose a masonry fireplace, it can be designed to incorporate a grill, a pizza oven, and even a crane that will support a kettle for soups and stews.

With or without cooking capabilities, a fireplace adds polish and personality to a kitchen. Situate utilitarian fireplaces next to the stove for optimum usability. Other styles are best enjoyed near the eating space and within sight of the work area. Raising the hearth brings the fireplace opening up to viewing level for seated diners. But if floor space is limited, a floor-level hearth may be a better option.

For a Scandinavian-Northern European look, consider facing the fireplace with glazed tile as shown *above right*. To create a Southwestern look, choose an adobe surround glazed to look centuries old. For more decorating punch, choose a stone-clad surround, or use tiles with exuberant patterns or bright solid colors.

ABOVE: **In full view of the kitchen island, this tile-clad surround encourages family members to congregate with the cook.**

OPPOSITE: **Applewood fires in this kitchen fireplace give pizza and breads a great smoky flavor. An iron grate a few inches above the flames holds the foods in place.**

A fireplace in the kitchen encourages guests and family members to gather and converse with the cooks.

ABOVE: The high placement of this fireplace makes it visible for diners seated at the counter stools, and it's a convenient height for cooking.

RIGHT: Angling the kitchen island provides fabulous views to the outdoors and keeps the tall, stone-surrounded fireplace in view.

Bedroom

In the bedroom, all of our romantic notions about a fireplace intensify: It is soothing and inspiring; it draws us out of the everyday and sets us dreaming. A fireplace lends importance to a small bedroom and gives a spacious bedroom an air of intimacy.

The flicker of firelight can calm hard-edged contemporary decor or bestow a glamorous glow on the simplest of furnishings. Whether your style calls for rose-strewn wallpaper and lace-edged sheets or a cool blue-and-white palette, this private retreat should set a mood that makes you comfortable. For maximum enjoyment, align your bed to give you the best view of the fireplace and fill in the remaining floor space with additional furnishings and accessories. If there's room, add a fireside chair (two is better) or a loveseat. For an added romantic touch, top the mantel with a fresh or dried flower arrangement and a favorite piece of framed art or a collection of special souvenirs.

Make your bedroom fireplace as convenient as possible to use and

you're likely to enjoy it more often. While the ritual of bringing in logs, building a perfect fire with kindling, and stoking and poking it to keep it burning bright may add to the enjoyment of a blaze in a family room fireplace, a wood-burning fireplace in the bedroom may seem like too much of a good thing. Instead, consider a gas fireplace with a remote control that you can turn on and off from under the covers.

While there is no one right spot for a bedroom fireplace, there are a number of practical and aesthetic considerations that can help you make the best decision. For example, in an upper-level bedroom, situating a fireplace to correspond with a hearth in the room below allows both to share the chimney structure, a substantial cost-cutting measure.

In a large bedroom you can create a fireplace wall to serve as a divider. Position the fireplace to face the bed to enclose the cozy sleeping area and you'll free the rest of the room for use as exercise or home office space. Use a see-through fireplace on the divider wall and you'll double its impact and enjoyment. For more information on using fireplaces as room dividers, see pages 78–79.

To maintain floor space in a small bedroom, consider tucking a fireplace into a corner. Southwestern-style fireplaces, as shown *opposite,* are often installed this way; factory-built models specifically designed for corners are also available.

If you have a bedroom where every inch of available wall space is taken up with doors, windows, and indispensable furniture, give the fireplace a room of its own. Anchored by a fireplace, a

small sitting room adjacent to the master bedroom can be a haven of privacy in a hectic household. Whether the bedroom and sitting room are open to each other or physically separated, give them a strong visual link by using a common color scheme and similar patterns and fabrics in each room.

ABOVE: **Create a natural focal point in your suite by installing a fireplace surround made of native stone. This river rock surround adds inviting texture to the Cape Cod-style room.**

OPPOSITE: **The clean simplicity of the Southwestern-style fireplace provides an eye-pleasing contrast to the room's more traditional furnishings.**

Flickering firelight imparts a touch of romance to a master suite. To control the fire without ever leaving the covers, install a remote-controlled gas unit.

BELOW: To increase function and storage, surround a bedroom fireplace with drawers and bookshelves. Here, doors above the direct-vent **gas-log** fireplace hold a large-screen television.

RIGHT: A decorative paint finish gives any vintage surround a fresh new face. Here, cream-color paint and a coffee-color glaze bring out the fine detailing of the surround in this master bedroom fireplace.

Bathroom

Step into that deep tub, sink into that bubble-filled paradise, and soon you're soaking away every major problem and minor ache. Now what could possibly make this sybaritic experience even more soul-soothing? The flickering flame of a fireplace, of course.

Because most bathrooms run the short gamut from very small to not very big, they lend themselves to dramatic decorating schemes dotted with a limited number of luxurious accessories. Materials that might be too grand or too expensive to use in a larger space are perfectly suited to a bathroom. You'll get lots of impact from any decorative efforts you put into this room—including a fireplace.

OPPOSITE: This fireplace was once part of a spare bedroom; a remodeling transformed the room into a spacious master bath. A new tumbled-marble surround and white painted mantel freshened the fireplace. Also, note how the abundant spread of branches and leaves make ferns the perfect choice for filling a firebox in the off season.

RIGHT: During the winter months, a glowing fire makes soaking in this tub feel especially indulgent. Again, a fern adds interest during the summer months.

Fireplaces and Plumbing Installing a fireplace in a bathroom requires careful planning and professional expertise. Whether you're remodeling or building, be sure the fireplace is on the agenda as decisions are made about placing the tub, shower, sinks, and toilet. Plan carefully to ensure plumbing lines, gas lines, and chimney flues all fit within the space. Check your local building codes as some municipalities have tighter restrictions than others. Address any specific code issues during planning to reduce the possibility of errors and costly modifications.

Shared Spaces

A double-sided fireplace offers a sleek and stylish way to divide gathering spaces or private quarters into separate activity areas while enabling both rooms to benefit from the warmth and the beauty of dancing flames from a single source.

If you'd love to have a fireplace in a room that you don't use all the time, a well-placed two-sided model may be the answer. In the formal Victorian dining room *opposite top*, the mirror above a double-sided fireplace mimics the shape of the flanking archways. The cost of a fireplace for the dining room alone might have been prohibitive, but being able to use it in two rooms made economic sense. That's often the thinking used when installing a fireplace between a bed and bath or bed and sitting room.

And, since fireplaces radiate heat in all directions, there's an additional economic benefit; you can add heat to two rooms with a single fireplace installed in a wall between the rooms.

RIGHT: **Installed in a partial wall, this double-sided fireplace vents through the ceiling and makes both the sleeping area and sitting area of the master bedroom feel more intimate.**

OPPOSITE TOP: **The repeated arch motif accentuates the feeling of connectedness between the dining room and adjacent parlor.**

OPPOSITE BELOW: **This double-sided fireplace warms both the master bath and the seating area of a master bedroom.**

See-Through Savvy See-through fireplaces share their warmth and charm with two rooms and are considerably less expensive than installing two separate fireplaces. A direct-vent or ventless fireplace unit makes it possible to create a partial wall or peninsula with a double-sided fireplace. To ensure privacy, avoid installing a double-sided fireplace between a home's public and private areas, as the firebox is open to both rooms. For more information about the different types of fireplaces, see Chapter 3.

Lower Level

For many families with growing pains, the search for more living space ends right under their feet. The basement holds precious square footage that with careful planning can be transformed into an attractive and comfortable living space.

Whether you call the final result a recreation room, den, or second family room, adding a fireplace or stove goes a long way toward dispelling the perception of a lower level room as a dark, damp, uninviting space. Because there are a number of special considerations when installing a hearth into a lower-level space, spend some time researching your options and understanding the air quality and moisture conditions of your basement.

Solve any moisture problems first. While a fireplace or stove does pick up moisture in a damp basement, the heated air will rise through the house, depositing condensation on cooler flue surfaces in the upper levels, substantially shortening the life of your flue. And replacing a flue from the basement all the way out through the roof is an expensive proposition!

Especially for a basement, it pays to bring in a pro. When you begin planning, consult a fireplace professional about the best options for basement-level heating. Be ready to share the size of the space, the number and size of any window openings, and the size and placement of any existing structures. Decide ahead of time what you want the fireplace or stove to contribute to the new space: Is it there mainly for aesthetics or do you want to use it as a heat source? A naturally drafted

masonry fireplace will give you gorgeous flames to look at but may actually draw warm air from the space. Vent-free appliances offer a secondary heat source but are not designed to provide round-the-clock heat.

If you have a gas-fired heating system and the home's mechanicals are in the basement, you have a gas line and a flue already in place that may make a gas-fueled fireplace an easy choice. In a cold climate, putting a fireplace on an outside wall and running a long chimney up the side of the house may not be the best solution. The chimney stays cold and may even freeze, especially if the fireplace is not used on a regular basis. This makes it difficult for the fireplace to heat the air in the chimney, and so it fails to draw properly.

ABOVE: **A wood-burning fireplace warms this lower level recreation room. The big-screen television (just out of view to the left) and wet-bar make it the perfect place to spend an afternoon watching sports.**

OPPOSITE: **A brass-and-steel firescreen gives this simple fireplace design a dash of visual interest and plays up the lines of the tile surround and flooring. The adjacent built-in cabinetry holds the television, media equipment, books, and board games.**

Whether your outdoor fireplace is part of a grand architectural facade or a simple fire pit in the backyard, it will extend your time spent in the great outdoors.

Outdoors

Too often, porches, patios, and sunrooms are limited to use only on fair weather days. Install a fireplace and instantly you have extended the season. When warmed by a fire, cool nighttime temperatures no longer deter patio dining or late-night stargazing. Guests and family members just gather a little closer to the flames.

If you have an existing indoor fireplace that's situated along an outside wall, you may be able to install an outdoor fireplace that backs up to it and shares its chimney.

Place your outdoor fireplace in an area with easy access to the interior spaces where you normally entertain, and guests will naturally gravitate to your new outdoor entertaining space. French doors that open from a living room or dining room to a porch or

The massive chimney and oversize fireplace are the focal points of this home's rear facade. The super-size proportions work well with the long, covered porch. At night a glowing fire helps illuminate the entire porch.

Year-Round Fun Time spent around an outdoor fireplace is so pleasant that many people install one even when they live in a climate where summers arrive late and leave early. Extend the quality fireside season by sheltering your hearth in an enclosed porch or a roofed space. Don't hesitate to continue entertaining in this enticing space even when the weather turns cold. Guests will bundle up with enthusiasm for a chili supper served at the fireside or for a cup of hot chocolate and marshmallows toasted over an open fire. An outdoor hearth is sure to become a favorite gathering spot. For more information about outdoor fireplaces, see page 108.

patio not only lend sparkle to the outdoor space, but also add panache to the interior. Be sure to place a generously sized doormat outside this door.

In addition to more substantial furniture, provide your outdoor fireside with plenty of lightweight seating and small tables that can easily be moved closer to or farther from the fire. Don't skimp on cushions and pillows, but be sure they're covered with a fabric that stands up to weather and hard use.

Low-level lighting enhances the atmosphere without competing with the firelight. Candles are a natural choice and are especially effective in large numbers: Cluster them on the mantel and on nearby tables. Outline the perimeter of the patios or the path that leads to it with simple luminarias. Discreet light fixtures in your yard and garden draw the attention of fireside sitters to distant trees and plantings.

Enhance the area around the fireplace with plants, flowers, and trees in pots that can be regrouped, changed with the season, or moved indoors when necessary. For a more ambitious project consider flanking the fireplace with brick or stone planters.

Since your outdoor hearth area is an extension of your home, you may want to keep its decor in sync with your interior, particularly if the area is within view of the inside. If your outdoor room is somewhat isolated, give it the feel of a vacation getaway by using a tropical or European design scheme.

ABOVE: **Adjacent to the breakfast room, this covered side porch is the perfect place to enjoy a morning cup of coffee or tea. When the weather is too warm to light a fire, potted plants fill the firebox.**

OPPOSITE: **This large fireplace provides a focal point for the outdoor gathering room and makes dining alfresco comfortable even on chilly evenings. The hearth and surround are made of heavy slate, while the bulk of the fireplace and outdoor kitchen are built with Italian terra-cotta pavers.**

Chapter 3

Alternative Options

Choosing the right kind of fireplace for your project is a complex decision. You'll need to determine what type of installation will best match your needs and your budget, as well as the type of fuel you'll want to burn. Here is a comprehensive comparison of the types of fireplaces currently on the market.

Wood-Burning Fireplaces

Wood-burning fireplaces can either be built on-site by a stonemason or purchased as a prefabricated unit. The aroma of burning wood, the crackling sounds, and the glow of the fire make these fireplaces attractive to homeowners. This type of fireplace can also be used to supplement heating. The drawbacks include cleaning up ashes and soot, and purchasing and storing firewood; buying wood by the cord can be as expensive as purchasing propane or natural gas.

• **Masonry fireplaces.** Custom-built fireplaces, also known as masonry fireplaces, are the most expensive fireplaces to install, but they can be designed to meet most any specifications. Available for centuries, these fireplaces remain a popular choice for higher-priced custom homes and historic renovations, particularly when paired with a gas starter. To build a basic brick masonry fireplace with a

4×3-foot firebox opening and a 20-foot-tall chimney, plan to spend from $6,000 to $8,500. The brick, stones, and concrete required to build a custom unit will also require more structural support than a prefabricated unit, adding to the overall cost.

Open wood-burning fireplaces, as shown on page 92, introduce small amounts of smoke and other emissions

LEFT: A modern insert outfitted with a period-style front made this old wood-burning fireplace much more efficient without negatively impacting its charm.

ABOVE: This wood-burning prefabricated fireplace enables you to view the flames from two sides and is ideal for homes with open floor plans.

Masonry Fireplace Components

Masonry fireplaces are made up of the components shown in the illustration *right*.

- The *firebox* is the open area that contains the fire. In masonry fireplaces this box is lined with firebrick, a type of masonry specially manufactured to withstand intense fires. In prefabricated fireplaces the firebox is lined with metal or a refractory material that looks like masonry bricks but is lighter in weight.
- The *hearth* technically refers to the floor of the fireplace; the term is also used to refer to the entire fireplace. The back hearth is the bottom of the firebox. The front hearth extends a short distance into the interior of a room and is usually covered with a decorative and fireproof material such as brick, stone, or tile.
- The *throat* is the area directly above the firebox and below the flue. This narrow opening allows the hot air and smoke to gain speed as they enter the flue, creating a draft that keeps the fire burning properly and prevents smoke from entering the room.
- The *damper* is the movable metal flap covering the throat; it is opened and closed manually. The open damper allows the fire to burn and smoke to escape. When the fire is out, the damper should be closed to prevent warm inside air from flowing up and out the chimney.
- The *smoke chamber* is the space directly above the throat. This prevents downdrafts in which outside air flows down into the firebox and causes smoke to flow into the room. Also, the smoke recirculates in this area so that ash particles are thoroughly burned before going up the chimney. The flat bottom of the smoke chamber is called the *smoke shelf*.
- The *flue* is the inside of the chimney. In today's fireplaces, flues are lined with heat-resistant interlocking clay or ceramic tiles, insulated metal pipe, or cast-in-place, heat-resistant concrete. The *liner* protects the chimney walls from heat and corrosion. A cast-in-place concrete liner is especially effective for repairing an older chimney because it helps ensure the structural integrity of aged bricks and mortar.
- A *cap* is installed at the top of the chimney. It keeps rain from entering the chimney where it could mix with soot to create acidic compounds that corrode the flue lining. A cap also helps prevent downdrafts in particularly windy conditions. A cap should sit at least 12 inches above the end of the chimney opening.
- An *ash pit*, a chamber situated below the fireplace, is an option for masonry fireplaces. Opening a small metal door in the floor of the firebox allows ashes to be swept into the ash pit. A clean-out door is located below the fireplace, often in the basement, for ash removal.

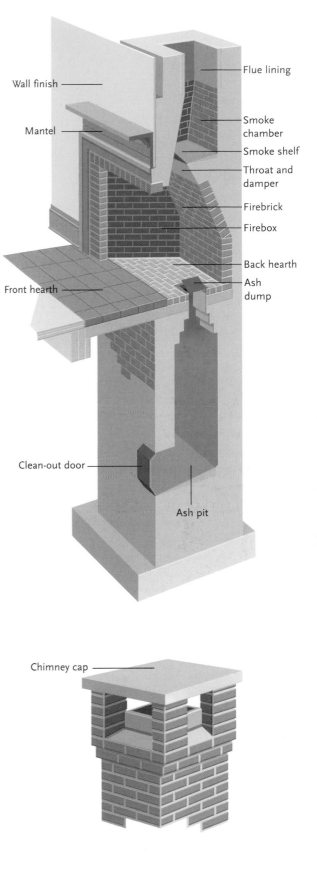

89

LEFT: It's all in the style. The rustic metal front on this gas insert maintains the fireplace's lodge-style look, keeping a secret of the new, easier to maintain workings.

BELOW: A simply designed wood-burning fireplace complements the Arts and Crafts styling of this living room.

into a home's interior, reducing indoor air quality as opposed to sealed gas units. For more information on air quality and fireplaces, see *Clearing the Air*, *opposite*. For more information about masonry fireplace installation requirements see the section *Masonry Fireplace Components*, on page 89. And for the various construction methods of masonry fireplaces, see *Masonry Fireplace Types*, on page 93.

• **Prefabricated wood-burning fireplaces.** Made from either cast iron or heavy-gauge steel, these straightforward metal fireplaces fit in relatively small spaces and are much easier to install than masonry fireplaces. Like their masonry counterparts, manufactured fireplaces include a throat and damper, a smoke chamber and shelf, and a chimney and flue. These components are designed to work together, so a prefabricated firebox engineered as part of this system should not be attached to an existing chimney. Instead choose a fireplace insert designed to work with existing components as discussed on page 91. Factory-built wood-burning units must be EPA-certified to meet both heating-

efficiency and air-quality standards. These fireplaces also include hookups for drawing outside air for combustion, a feature that makes them extremely energy efficient. Clean-face prefabricated fireplaces, as shown *below right*, eliminate the black metal surround often associated with factory-built fireplaces and make it difficult to tell the difference between prefabricated and custom-made fireplaces. Expect to pay from $800 to $5,000 depending on the size and the features of the model you choose. Add $1,200 to $1,800 for installation.

• **Prefabricated insert.** Similar to stand-alone factory-made fireplaces, prefabricated inserts are designed to upgrade old masonry fireplaces without giving up the look, sound, and fragrance of a natural wood fire. These inserts are designed to fit completely inside an existing masonry fireplace opening or to protrude slightly—a design feature that allows more heat to radiate into the room.

An insert does not include a chimney system and must be connected to an existing chimney with a special sealed collar. You may also need a chimney liner to resize the flue. Inserts are heavy, weighing from 600 to 1,000

RIGHT: Today's wood-burning fireplaces come in all shapes and sizes. This contemporary orb-shape fireplace is made from 10-gauge steel and suspends from the ceiling via a stainless steel chimney.

BELOW: This prefabricated wood-burning fireplace costs much less than a custom-built masonry one and is much easier to install. A variety of door options makes it a good fit for most any architectural or decorating style.

pounds, and installation is critical to ensure proper functioning of the fireplace, so professional installation is recommended. A top-quality insert costs between $1,200 and $2,500 depending on the size and the options you select.

Masonry Fireplace Types

There are three basic configurations of wood-burning masonry fireplaces that are still being built today:

• The Rumford fireplace is the forebear of the modern fireplace. It is named for Count Rumford, a Massachusetts-born scientist whose 18th-century work was primarily concerned with the nature of heat. Rumford fireplaces have shallower fireboxes—just 18 to 20 inches deep—rounded throats, sidewalls angled at 45 degrees, and upright, vertical backs. The shallow firebox and angled sidewalls are designed to radiate more heat toward interior rooms, while the straight back allows smoke and gases to exit directly into the flue.

• The Orton fireplace is named after Vrest Orton, author of the 1969 book, *The Forgotten Art of Building Good Fireplaces*. Orton's design pitched the back wall of the firebox forward slightly to better reflect heat toward living spaces. Because the slanted back would sometimes allow smoke to drift into interiors, Orton compensated by creating a straight throat that ensured a powerful draw and eliminated smoke infiltration.

• The modern fireplace features a steeply pitched back wall, and a throat positioned well forward to the flue. This design forces smoke and hot gases to rotate just before entering the flue, ensuring complete combustion inside the firebox. Generally this design does not radiate heat as effectively as the Rumford or Orton.

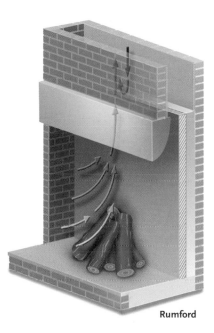

Rumford

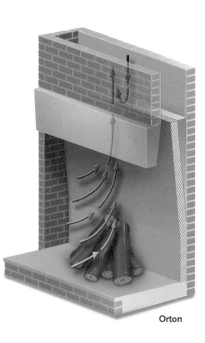

Orton

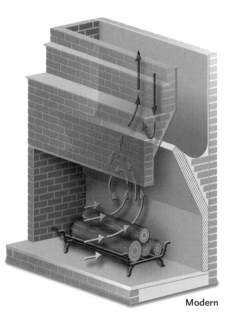

Modern

Gas-Burning Fireplaces

Cleaner burning and more energy efficient than their wood-burning counterparts, gas fireplaces also offer the convenience of turning on and off with the flip of a switch or the push of a button. These fireplaces eliminate the need to gather and store wood and clean out ashes. Many include a remote-controlled thermostat so that they can be cycled on and off to maintain a specific room temperature. There are several different types of gas-burning fireplaces:

• **Gas direct-vent fireplaces.** These fireplaces eliminate the need for a chimney and flue so they are easier and less expensive to install. The vent doesn't need to run vertically up through the roof like a chimney. Instead a short section of horizontal pipe exits through a wall so that these units can be installed most anywhere—such as under windows or as a room divider. On the sealed-glass-front models, all of the air needed for combustion comes from outside the home. One hundred percent of the exhaust is expelled back

Prefabricated fireplaces are available in a variety of shapes and sizes to fit most any space.

ABOVE: **This direct-vent fireplace features an arched design and a masonry-look interior that eliminates the louvers and other distractions common in older models of gas fireplaces. This particular model features brushed nickel bun-warming doors that offer direct access to the flames.**

OPPOSITE: **This B-vent fireplace displays the black metal surround commonly found on many gas fireplace models. The see-through model is set into the wall between a master bath and bedroom, providing a tranquil and romantic ambience in each room.**

outdoors, so the units do not interfere with indoor air quality. These sealed fireplaces are also extremely energy efficient; some are even rated as furnaces. They may be fitted with traditional masonry or wood surrounds so they look very much like traditional wood-burning fireplaces. Low- and moderately priced models may have black metal frames and black metal interiors, as shown *opposite*. Upgraded models, as shown *above*, now offer a "clean face" appearance that eliminates the black frame and includes a firebrick-look interior. A few direct-vent

models also include a halogen bulb that emulates the glow of embers to suggest the ambience of a fire without ever turning on the gas.

The sealed-glass panel on most direct-vent fireplaces prevents easy access to the flames, so the units can't be used for roasting marshmallows or popping popcorn. Some models offer optional hinged doors to provide flame access. A few manufacturers also make direct-vent models that are open to the room. Though they do use a small amount of inside air for combustion, they pull the greater share of that

air from the outdoors, offering greater heating efficiency and better indoor air quality than many other fireplaces. For a quality gas direct-vent fireplace expect to pay between $1,000 and $6,000.

• **Gas B-vent and top-vent fire-places.** Unlike direct-vent fireplaces, these gas fireplace models are not sealed from the room. Gas flames can be accessed through movable glass doors or a metal mesh curtain. Because they use indoor air for combustion, these fireplaces are less efficient than their sealed counterparts and may

allow some gases and smoke to filter into the inside air. They are priced similarly to direct-vent models.

• **Gas vent-free or room-vented fire-places.** As the names imply, vent-free fireplaces, also referred to as room-vented fireplaces, do not require special venting or air ducts for safe operation. The burners are designed to reduce carbon monoxide during combustion, allowing them to be installed virtually anywhere. Although these units meet federal safety and emissions standards, 13 states currently restrict or ban their

use. Concerns include the use of these stoves in small rooms or extremely air-tight locations where they may deplete oxygen to unsafe levels. For safety, manufacturers of these appliances include an oxygen-depletion detector— a switch that automatically shuts off the appliance if the oxygen falls below safe levels.

Another concern is moisture which can eventually lead to mold growth. Instead of drying out the air, as many people expect a fire to do, a vent-free appliance actually produces a quart or

The gas logs in today's gas fireplaces can be unbelievably realistic—or abominably fake. Unfortunately, not all gas fireplaces offer a choice of logs, so be sure to check which logs come with the unit you are considering before making a purchase. Some systems offer different wood choices as well as flexible log placement. Others include glowing embers and a slow shut off that emulates the look of logs burning out naturally. Whatever log choice you make, be sure the gas pipe is well-hidden. The flames should appear in a random pattern similar to a wood-burning fire and be tall and bright enough to fill the firebox.

OPPOSITE: **Designed to fit in smaller spaces, this double-sided direct-vent fireplace is perfect for bedrooms and sitting areas. It also features a clean face and a brick-look interior.**

BELOW: **This wood-burning fireplace is fitted with a gas starter that can be turned on and off with the flip of a switch enabling you to start the logs burning with very little effort.**

more of water vapor per hour. To prevent unwanted condensation these units need to be properly sized to the room and if necessary, a portable dehumidifier installed in the room. Because they have fewer parts and are easier to install than other gas models, you can purchase these fireplaces for as little as $800.

• **Gas fireplace inserts.** Similar to wood-burning fireplace inserts, gas inserts are designed to make an old

masonry fireplace heat better while using less energy, and burn gas instead of wood. The inserts are designed to fit completely inside an existing masonry fireplace opening or to protrude slightly—as noted, to allow more heat to radiate into the room. An insert does not include a chimney system and must be connected to an existing chimney with a special sealed collar. You may also need a chimney liner to

resize the flue. A top-quality insert costs from $1,200 to $4,000 depending on the size and options.

• **Gas log inserts.** Installing a gas line and a set of gas logs inside an existing masonry fireplace gives you all the convenience of a gas fireplace with little remodeling expense. To have a gas line installed, contact your local gas provider for an estimate or for a list of qualified contractors. If you already have a gas furnace, adding a second line to the main floor of your home is usually a simple operation. If you have to run lines through interior walls or up the side of your home to a second floor, the cost goes up dramatically. As with other gas fireplace options, gas logs produce a clean burn, there are no ashes to clean

OPPOSITE TOP: **This unusual sealed-glass cylinder gas fireplace features a whirling flame and a 360-degree view of the fire.**

OPPOSITE BOTTOM: **A small opening and a narrow depth enable this single-sided direct-vent gas fireplace to fit into a small space.**

ABOVE: **Its clean-faced glass front makes this arch-shaped direct-vent gas fireplace look nearly identical to a masonry fireplace.**

LEFT: **A bronze metal face frame adds a decorative touch to this direct-vent gas fireplace.**

up, and you can turn the fire on and off with a switch or button. Gas logs, however, are not nearly as energy efficient as direct-vent gas fireplaces and can be somewhat expensive to operate. Gas log sets cost from $250 to $500. Because the inside air is open to the fire, combustion gases may adversely affect indoor air quality.

This see-through gas fireplace vents through a chimney, much like a wood-burning fireplace. Leaving the flue exposed adds to the industrial look of this loft.

Get double the mileage out of a new fireplace by installing a see-through model that can be viewed from both sides of a large room.

Alternative-Fuel Fireplaces

Pellet Fireplaces

Pellet fuel is made from recycled sawdust compressed under great pressure to form hard nuggets about the size of small marbles. Typically sold in 40-pound bags, the pellets are available from some home centers and hardware stores (check your local stores to see if they are available in your area) and cost about the same to burn as standard logs. Pellet flames resemble cordwood flames; however, pellets burn with greater efficiency and produce less smoke and soot than traditional cordwood fires.

Appliances that burn pellet fuel are available as freestanding stoves and fireplace inserts. Both versions use an electric mechanism to deliver the pellets to the burning chamber at a rate determined by a thermostat. Most do not require chimneys; they vent through a sidewall in a fashion similar to direct-vent gas fireplaces. Expect to pay from $1,250 to $3,000 for a quality pellet-burning appliance. Pellets can be burned in wood-burning fireplaces, but you will need to purchase a special pellet basket. You can find these baskets online or special order them from some fireplace retailers.

Gel Fireplaces

For a low-maintenance occasional evening fire, gel-fuel fireplaces are a viable option. These freestanding units do not require a chimney, a vent, or electricity. Sold as a complete unit, including mantel, surround, and firebox, these fireplaces are fueled by cans of alcohol-based gel that's similar to the fuel often used under buffet serving dishes. (Decorative ceramic logs hide the fuel can.) The cost of a can of fuel is about $1 per hour of burn time; most people burn two or three cans at once. The fuel can be shut down and saved for another burn by replacing the can lid. Most gel-based fireplaces cost from $300 to $1,200 depending on the complexity of the hearth surround and mantelpiece. Check with your local municipality to see if these fireplaces are allowed in your area.

ABOVE: **This corner-fit freestanding gel fireplace comes complete with ceramic logs and a cherry surround. Flat wall models are also available. Similar units are priced from $650 to $1,000.**

OPPOSITE: **This electric fireplace creates the ambience of a fire inside a high-rise condominium. The granite tile surround, maple hearth, and decorative glass doors make it a focal point.**

Electric Fireplaces

Electric fireplaces, which run on standard household current, and are ideal for retrofit situations or for apartments, condominiums, or other locations where wood- or gas-burning appliances may be prohibited. Like standard fireplaces these freestanding units feature mantels, hearths, decorative surrounds, and "fireboxes." Better models feature imitation flames that sway and flicker, similar to a wood fire. Lightweight woodstove look-alikes are also available.

Some electric fireplaces separate heating elements and flames so you can use the unit as a space heater without displaying flames, or display flames without heating the room. If you plan to use the unit as a space heater, be sure to choose a model with variable heat settings to maintain a comfortable room temperature. Prices range from less than $600 to $3,000 depending on the size of the unit and the complexity of the hearth surround and mantelpiece.

Wood-Burning and Gas Stoves

If heating efficiency is important to you, consider a freestanding stove. Today's wood-burning models are more energy efficient than ever before. Advanced combustion technology reduces emissions while increasing the amount of heat transferred to your home. This efficient combustion also burns up pollutants that once would have entered the atmosphere.

Be sure to select a stove designed for your particular room size. Choosing too large or small a stove reduces energy efficiency and can cause unnecessary condensation. Look for stoves made of plate steel or cast iron at least $\frac{1}{4}$-inch thick. Better models have a "window wash" feature that blows air across the inside of the glass to keep it free of soot.

Stoves also are manufactured in gas- and oil-burning models. Like their wood-burning counterparts, these stoves tend to be highly efficient and clean-burning due to strict EPA standards imposed in the last decade.

You may also want to consider a wood-burning stove that provides radiant heat by warming a soapstone exterior. This European soapstone stove, *opposite*, soaks up enough heat from a two-hour fire to radiate warmth for up to 24 hours. Incorporating a baking oven lets the heat do double duty. Note that this natural stone is extremely heavy, so you will need to reinforce floor joists before installing a large heater like this one. Smaller, lighter-weight models are also available.

ABOVE: **This wood-burning porcelain stove is as beautiful as it is efficient. A non-combustible hearth pad is not required; however, the floor beneath the stove must be level and strong enough to support the stove without a tipping hazard. If installed over carpet or vinyl flooring, a metal-, ceramic tile-, or wood-panel that extends the full width and depth of the stove must be installed.**

ABOVE RIGHT: **This simple cast-iron gas stove blends the charm of yesteryear with the technology of today. It has an 80-percent-plus efficiency rating and is available in three different sizes to fit most rooms. Options include a variety of color choices, remote control, thermostat, and a fan kit.**

OPPOSITE: **This freestanding soapstone-clad wood-burning stove is an ideal room divider; see-through doors enable you to see the fire from both sides. A bake oven is perfect for pizzas and crusty breads.**

More Options

You can create the look of a fireplace with less expense by simply building or buying a realistic-looking surround and then filling the unvented firebox with pillar or votive candles instead of logs. Or stack a narrow stone grate with logs to make it appear as if you were moments away from lighting a fire—just be sure an unsuspecting guest never decides to light it!

You can purchase vintage surrounds at flea markets, antiques shops, and architectural salvage warehouses. Choose a model that fits your available space and style and nail it in place.

Check home improvement centers for packaged mantel kits. These ready-to-assemble projects similar to the one shown *opposite* come in a limited number of styles and sizes, but the ready-cut pieces and assembly instructions make them a convenient shortcut.

Still can't find what you want? Flip through the pages of this book and home decorating magazines to find a mantel style you like. Duplicate it using individual molding pieces from a lumberyard or home improvement center. Add your own touches to take do-it-yourself to the creative level of design-it-yourself.

Remember that the most eye-pleasing mantels complement both the architectural style of the home and its interior design. To make your new mantel look as if it had always been a part of your home, choose trim pieces that match those found elsewhere in your house such as on door or window moldings. If your cabinetry has a rope trim or an elaborate crown, create a similar look for your mantel. For a more realistic appearance, trim the wall surrounding the firebox with ceramic or stone tiles. For more information on mantel design and decorating, see Chapter 4.

BELOW: Set a warm tone for your decorating scheme by installing a real mantel embellished by a trompe l'oel painted tile surround complete with a crackling fire .

OPPOSITE: If you long for the flicker of real flames, install a brick-look inset below a traditional mantel and fill it with soft-glowing candles.

Fireplace Candles

Whatever the season outside, you can add a warm glow to a dark firebox with a display of stout candles. Look for wrought iron, pewter, and other metal candle racks or candle "trees" in mail-order catalogs, home decorating stores, and candle shops. These multi-arm stands hold 6 to 12 pillar candles in staggered rows. You can also create your own display without a ready-made candleholder. Avoid placing candles directly on the hearth. Instead, rest each on a heat-proof base of metal, glass, or brick to catch the drippings. Follow these tips to keep your glowing display of candles safe:

- Limit the number of candles. Too many candles can overheat the firebox.
- If your fireplace is operable, open the flue and the glass doors. Otherwise, move the candles toward the front of the firebox.
- For safety, place a decorative metal firescreen in front of the candles.
- Be sure the room is adequately ventilated; candles use a surprisingly large amount of oxygen.
- Keep a fire extinguisher on hand.
- Never leave burning candles unattended.

Outdoor Fireplace Options

There's something both primitive and luxurious about an outdoor fire. Recently, various freestanding products have appeared that bring to your backyard the camaraderie of a campfire and the romance of a full-blown fireplace. You can choose from hefty 6-foot-tall steel, stone, or faux stone fireplaces meant to remain where you place them, to portable 3-foot-tall models that can be wheeled to wherever they're needed. Many municipalities have ordinances that prohibit outdoor open burning of any kind, so check with your local government before investing in any of these options.

Inexpensive and widely available terra-cotta chimneas also offer inexpensive ways to bring firelight to any

ABOVE: **This open-air gas-powered fire pit brings the beauty of a campfire to your patio without the hassle of cleaning up ashes or lugging firewood.**

Light up the night with an outdoor hearth that brings the cheer and charm of the campfire to your own backyard.

This outdoor wood-burning fireplace is built much like an interior fireplace would be. A gas starter enables the owners to start a fire in seconds.

fireproof outdoor surface. These curvaceous stand-alone fireplaces are made of a clay body set within a metal stand. Some models include caps or screens to keep rain, debris, and small animals out when not in use. Chimneas range from 2 to 6 feet tall. The smaller ones work well on balconies or small patios. Bigger models can heat larger outdoor gathering spaces.

Other readily available outdoor hearth products include wok-shape open fire pits, rectangular or square wood-burning metal-framed stoves, and portable wheeled units in a variety of shapes that offer an optional grill. Some gas-, oil- and gel-fueled models are also available. You can find most of these outdoor products at patio shops and home centers as well as at fireplace dealers. Gardening supply catalogs also feature stylish patio options. Or do an online search for outdoor fireplaces.

OPPOSITE: Made from poured concrete, this wood-burning firepit features a sand bottom fitted with an iron fireplace grate.

BELOW: This unusual see-through fireplace combines fireplace and window. It installs on the exterior wall of a home, enabling the owners to enjoy the beauty of the fire from both the inside and outside.

Chapter 4

Decorating a Fireplace

One of the pleasures—and challenges—of having a fireplace is decorating it and the spaces around it. The prospect of producing a pleasing arrangement for this prominent spot in your home may leave you feeling like an artist standing before a blank canvas: eager to begin, and a bit daunted too. These decorating tips should help make the process an easy and enjoyable one.

Material Matters

Once you've determined what type of fireplace you want, it's time to make design decisions regarding the material and color selections for the hearth, the surround (also referred to as the facing), and the mantel area.

Fireplace hearths and surrounds need to be covered with a fireproof material. Material requirements vary depending on the type and size of fireplace you choose as well as local building codes, so check with your municipality's building department before finalizing any plans.

Hearth and Surround Options

The following materials are excellent choices for both the hearth and surround. They're all fireproof, but each has a unique visual appeal.

• **Stone and rock.** Granite, marble, soapstone, limestone, and other natural stones and rocks provide timeless styling. The surfaces, whether cut and sanded into smooth slabs or left in their natural state, stand up to heat and bring natural beauty and color to any fireplace facing or hearth. Solid colors with shiny finishes have a tendency to show ashes and fingerprints. To reduce upkeep, consider a variegated stone with a rough or honed finish. If you

RIGHT: **A simple black metal fireplace surround keeps the focus of the hearth wall on the rows of framed prints. To create a similar art arrangement in your home, plan the arrangement on paper, drawing the wall to scale to determine the best spacing. Here, the prints are spaced 6 inches above the fireplace with 3 inches between each print.**

TOP: An old-fashioned raised brick hearth and fireplace surround complements the casual country styling of this gathering area. A white painted wooden mantel set into an arched niche filled with open shelves frames the brick and prevents the elongated, curved hearth from appearing bottom-heavy.

ABOVE: A statuary marble surround and an ornate wooden mantel enhance the visual impact of this small fireplace in a living room. Flanking window seats of identical dimensions create a sense of balance, as does the formal mantel top display.

plan to use natural stone or rock to make up the mantel and/or overmantel, you will likely need extra structural support to bear the material's heavy weight. As an alternative, consider cultured stone. It looks and feels like natural rock, but weighs only about a quarter as much as natural stone.

• **Ceramic tile.** Ceramic tiles make an attractive and durable hearth and/or surround and are available in an array of colors, styles, and sizes. To disguise fingerprints and dust on this classic surfacing, choose a honed finish.

• **Brick.** Like tile, this surfacing option is attractive and durable, and it's a longtime traditional favorite for

LEFT: Wrapped in a stair-stepping partial wall that's painted cobalt blue, this custom-cut bronze metal surround adds fun to the room. Sleek black granite tiles accent the modern styling and serve the practical purpose of protecting the hearth floor.

ABOVE: Tumbled stone tiles laid in a basket-weave pattern and framed by 3-inch squares contrast against a cherry hearth in this lower level direct-vent gas fireplace.

the fireplace facing. A range of looks can be produced depending on the bricks you choose and the pattern in which you lay them. As with stone, if you plan to use bricks to cover a large portion of the fireplace wall, you may need extra structural support.

• **Engineered quartz.** Made from crushed quartz with binders, engineered quartz has a composition, weight, appearance, and price comparable to natural stone. Because it is nonporous and fireproof, this low-maintenance material makes an excellent fireplace surround. It is available in both tile and slab form.

• **Concrete.** Concrete surrounds are nearly as durable as granite. Hairline cracks are common, but do not affect the strength of the material. Wet concrete can be dyed virtually any color, and, before it is fully cured, can be stamped or embedded with decorative inlays to create any surface texture or appearance. Because concrete is very porous, it is often sealed for protection against dirt and stains.

• **Metal.** Surrounds made of metal may be sleek and contemporary, rustic and antique, or vintage reproductions. Options include bronze, copper, iron, nickel, or steel tiles.

Mantel Options

If the mantel is placed well above the firebox, it doesn't have to be fireproof and that allows you the most flexibility in material options. Because of its prominent position, the mantel is

OPPOSITE: **Rough-hewn limestone covers the fireplace surround, overmantel, and hearth in this casual gathering area. A thick, solid wood mantel punctuates the rustic facade without detracting from it.**

BELOW: **This exquisitely carved limestone facade is clearly classic, and fits well in this formal living room.**

A simple wooden mantel is the perfect accent for the rustic stone surround.

something you'll see every day—so don't make this choice in haste.

• **Wood.** Attractive, versatile, and easy to install, wood is the most common material choice for the mantel. New mantels can resemble vintage pieces with elaborate carvings and furniture detailing, or left purposely plain to complement a more contemporary or rustic motif.

• **Carved- or cast-stone.** Carved stone mantels such as the one shown on page 118 are elegant and timeless. They may be made of marble, limestone, granite, or slate, and are hand- or machine-carved. Cast stone versions replicate the look of natural stone but at a lower cost.

• **Concrete.** With it's rocklike color and malleable nature, concrete can simulate the look of a carved or cast stone but is lighter weight because the material is reinforced with fiberglass. As with the fireplace facing, custom looks can be achieved with different color and texture finishes.

• **Metal.** As with metal surrounds, metal mantels can be made from cast-bronze, copper, nickel, iron, or steel. Finishes include an aged verdigris or gilded. Look for metal mantels at fireplace shops specializing in custom mantel designs and online.

• **Plaster and Gypsum.** Poured in molds, these delicate mantels typically feature more intricate detailing than their wood counterparts and can be painted to replicate carved limestone, wood, or metal.

RIGHT: A grid of rustic green ceramic tiles lends a casual air to the fireplace in this den. Cherry paneling adorns the overmantel and mantelshelf to create a cozy and inviting ambience.

BELOW: Ceramic tiles adorned with blue and white hand-painted sailboats are an excellent choice for this quaint cottage room. A plain, solid mantel is the perfect complement.

Vintage Mantels If you enjoy antiquing you may find a vintage fireplace mantel at an architectural salvage yard or through an antiques dealer. If you can't find a perfect fit, it may be possible to cut a larger mantel down to size. Before installing an antique mantel, ask a design professional such as a licensed architect or certified designer to make sure the piece will meet your municipality's building code requirements.

Mantel Makeovers

The mantelshelf offers a changeable decorating platform. Any object you put there can be moved and replaced on a whim, changed with the seasons, or left in place for a lifetime.

Because the fireplace is often the focal point of a room, it is the perfect place for displaying the things that matter most to you, or just the things that bring a smile. Precious heirlooms qual-ify for mantel status, as do family photos and quirky finds. If you're a collector, display your treasures, such as birdhouses, seashells, hand-blown glass vases, or vintage picture frames. Vacation mementos make wonderful fireside companions too. Show off the giant pinecone from the north woods or the starfish the kids brought home from the shore. If it pleases you to see

LEFT: For an artistic decorating statement, stack a favorite framed print against a gilded framed mirror and then balance the arrangement with a colorful vase of fresh flowers on one side of the mantel and a smaller piece of art hung on the wall on the opposite side.

ABOVE: In lieu of more traditional choices that would match the style of surround, such as could give the mantel a garden-fresh look like this by adorning it with a row of potted plants and a contemporary framed print.

Pair the complexity of your mantel display with the intensity of the room's decor.

it every day, it will likely please your family and friends.

In summer, or whenever it's not in use, keep the firebox visually interesting by adding a decorative firescreen (a good choice because metal screens serve an important function during the cooler months as well) as shown on these pages, an arrangement of candles or birch branches, or a potted plant.

OPPOSITE: A vintage iron firescreen adds interest to the firebox, whether or not a fire is burning. You can purchase similar accessories at fireplace shops, antiques stores, home decor retailers, and online.

BELOW: A wooden mantel painted slate gray complements the natural slate tiles on this arch-topped fireplace. Because of the busy slate pattern and the simplicity of the rest of the room's decor, the mantel display is kept simple: a pair of iron candlesticks and a flowing tapestry.

If you love drama, consider displaying only one large painting.

Personal Style

Take a look around the room where your fireplace is or will be. Is the area filled with accessories or left purposely bare? If your matching love seats are peeping out from under a dozen chintz-covered throw pillows, chances are you'll lean toward the same feeling of abundance on the mantel. If, on the other hand, your sleek chrome-and-leather sofa stands in solitary splendor, you'll want to think about choosing a single important object to place above the fireplace.

Paper Trail

To ensure successful placement of artwork and accessories, start by tracing an outline on paper of whatever you plan to hang on the fireplace wall—a mirror, framed artwork, sconces, and

LEFT: **The architecture of this great room creates a necessity for fireplace simplicity. A single oil painting adorns the mantelshelf; the painting height draws attention to the grandeur of the vaulted ceiling, and extending the neutral-color shelf from wall to wall marks the width.**

ABOVE: **If your room is filled with other architectural amenities, such as this wall of arched-top windows, a minimal mantel display will prevent the room from feeling busy. Here, a single framed watercolor is centered atop a classic brick overmantel and the narrow mantelshelf was left bare.**

so on. Cut out and tape these shapes to the wall. This allows you to integrate the mantelshelf with the wall display, adjusting the paper shapes as necessary.

Whether you use a few objects or many on your mantel, you'll create the liveliest effect by introducing a variety of shapes, heights, and textures. Experiment by gathering a half dozen decorative items with a range of silhouettes—perhaps a pair of tall, slim candlesticks, some round china plates, a trailing plant in a chunky terra-cotta pot, and a stack of vintage books. Arrange them in varying ways on the mantel, changing their relationship to each other and the amount of space between them. Add or subtract objects

until you have a look you like. Ultimately, any "mantelscape" that pleases you is successful, but there are some guidelines that may help you to reach that point. When all the items you want to show are the same size, add interest by elevating some on decorative boxes or stacks of books. Layer items, with larger ones in the background, smaller ones up front. Give small collectibles impact by grouping them together. Look for a pleasing balance.

Remember to consider the scale of the room and the fireplace in relationship to the objects on display. A high ceiling may dwarf a delicate arrangement, while an oversize, bold painting can overwhelm a small fireplace.

ABOVE: **This set of framed prints offset by a pair of matching contemporary lamps and bronze sculptures give this very traditional fireplace a decidedly modern spin.**

OPPOSITE: **If you feel most comfortable when surrounded with an abundance of accessories, you'll likely enjoy a fireplace surrounded by an abundance of open shelves where you can display your favorite items and enjoy them every day. Here, a pair of potted ferns anchors a plentiful arrangement of vintage books and collectibles. Because most of the items on display are dark-colors, the built-in was painted white to create needed visual contrast.**

Balancing Act

More than creative genius enables designers to produce beautiful rooms. Underlying those impressive interiors are some basic design principles that you can use to shape your mantelscape. Among the most important is harmony. Plan the mantel to contribute to the room's harmony by reflecting the style and colors of the furnishings and fabrics around it.

Is your fireside chair casual, cottagey, or country style? Match its mood with similarly themed artwork and accessories. Follow the same rule of thumb with any style.

Keep mirror and picture frames appropriate to the overall style of the room. Don't introduce a new color on the mantel. Instead, echo one or more of the primary or secondary colors in the room.

Harmony needn't mean monotony. Vary the shapes, textures, and heights of objects on your mantel for a stylistic composition that's lively too.

OPPOSITE: Matching antique chairs and double doorways flanking the fireplace lend symmetry to this focal-point living room wall. For visual interest, vintage frames displayed on the mantel are propped slightly askew, while smaller Items harmonlously balance the display.

LEFT: A pair of ornate candlesticks balance a vase of fresh garden flowers in this simple mantel arrangement. The French painting centered between the groupings defines the accent colors for the room.

Balancing Scales
One of the easiest ways to determine if a mantel arrangement will look visually balanced is to picture in your mind the display items separated onto each side of an old-fashioned balancing scale. If in your mind's eye the scale balances, then the display will most likely appear balanced. If it doesn't balance, decide whether it's better to add an item to one side or to remove an item from the opposite side.

Color Around the Fireplace

Sometimes white is just right, but often it's the default choice, the neutral we choose when we're too timid to step to the paint counter and say, "Make mine Persian blue," or "Venetian red please, with a twist of lime." If you've always lived with white or off-white walls, a color change may seem like a big design decision. But chances are there's a color out there with your name on it. Ask yourself what character you want the room to have. Neutrals such as brown and gray connote elegance. Straight-ahead primary shades of blue and yellow send out cheerful vibrations. Red signals warmth, passion, and celebration.

One good way to choose a room's dominant color is to pick a color in a work of art, area rug, or fabric you plan to use in the room. Contrasting a bold wall color with a white mantel will spot-

OPPOSITE: **A cherry-red wall warms up this black-and-white mantel display of shadow boxes and picture frames. Although the arrangement is asymmetrical, careful placement of large and small items maintains visual balance.**

BELOW: **Champagne-color paneling adorns this fireplace facade, creating an ambience of serenity and romance. A large vintage mirror gives the fireplace wall character while adding depth by creating the illusion of a larger room.**

Coloring the fireplace wall accentuates the beauty of the surround.

light the fireplace. The same color paired with a natural wood-stained surround results in a sophisticated look that integrates the fireplace into the room. While saturated colors tend to energize, soft shades are almost always restful. If you want to create a fireside haven away from family activities or a retreat to come home to, temper your color choice by mixing plenty of white into whatever color you use.

To keep colors upbeat, opt for a base of warm yellow or red. To create a serene feeling, choose cool grays, soft blues, or sage greens—the colors you'll see in many spas. To add visual interest to a monochromatic scheme, underscore the color with a variety of textures and patterns.

To help narrow your color selections, visit a user-friendly paint store and ask to compare several shades of the color you have in mind. Note that paint colors can look very different depending on the finish. A high-gloss finish intensifies the color, but also shows every irregularity on a surface. Flat paint minimizes surface flaws, but absorbs light, dulling the color. For most rooms an eggshell or semigloss finish is just right.

Once you've found a color and finish you like, purchase a quart of the chosen paint and brush it onto several pieces of poster board. Stand the boards along each wall of the room you plan to paint and view the painted boards throughout the day and

evening; you may be surprised by how much the color "changes." Repeat the process with other shades until you find the right shade for your project.

OPPOSITE: **A crayon-green wall spotlights this simple arrangement of flower-filled glass cookie jars hung from colorful yellow ribbons, burlap runners adorned with ribbons and flower blossoms, and shiny aluminum planters filled with grass. In fall, the arrangement comes down and is replaced with dried floral arrangements and stacks of pillar candles.**

BELOW: **Flowers growing on a nearby vine inspired the coral-color walls surrounding this outdoor fireplace. It's a nice earthy choice for an outdoor room.**

Before and After Tales:

One of the best ways to see how the look of a fireplace can change the ambience of a room is to look at Before and After scenarios.

Simple Surround

The fireplace, *right,* was updated with a fireplace surround kit purchased from a fireplace shop. You can find similar kits in manufacturer's catalogs, online, and at fireplace shops in your area. To give the kit a custom look, consider adding paneling above the fireplace, as shown. The wall paneling above the mantel features the same molding design as the mantelshelf and sides, and was purchased from the same manufacturer as the fireplace surround.

Painting the surround the same color as the woodwork in the rest of your house will make the refurbished fireplace appear as if it had always been a part of your home. To create an elegant surround, choose a surfacing material in a shade similar to the painted surround. Here, 12-inch square cream and taupe marble tiles create an appearance similar to a single slab without the cost or difficult installation. Marble can be polished to a flat finish as shown.

RIGHT: **New marble tiles cover the original bricks on this fireplace surround. Made from a kit, the mantel and surround with paneling adds a classic touch to the prominent fireplace. Hearth tiles were laid on the diagonal for added interest.**

Cabinetry Encasement

The fireplace in this living room, *left,* was too big and heavy to be covered over with a mantel kit, but its rustic appearance looked out of place when paired with the rest of the homeowners' classic furnishings. To give the fireplace a more traditional appearance, the owners scrubbed off the soot that had collected on the stone facade over decades and flanked the surround in a classically styled frame of glass-fronted cherry cabinets.

To incorporate your fireplace into a wall of built-ins, add cabinets on each side of the surround that are deeper than the fireplace itself. A deep mantel can bridge between the new cabinets. For more visual connection, wrap the tops of the cabinets and the stone surround with additional molding. Rather than trying to overpower a massive facade with an elaborate design, keep the cabinetry simple. Here, flat recessed door panels create strong vertical lines that offset rather than compete with the strength of the stone. The choice of wood is important too; cherry's color stands up to the stone.

The built-ins had the bonus of adding display and storage space. Use open shelves or glass-fronted cabinets to show off collectibles and enclosed lower cabinets to house less-attractive audio-visual equipment.

Take care to update the lighting in the fireplace area by adding wall sconces or track lights. Here, the molding that runs across the top of the mantel hides recessed halogen fixtures that illuminate the mantel display.

LEFT: New built-ins and freshly cleaned stone make it difficult to believe that these fireplace photos are of the same stone surround.

Stone and Mortar

Before the makeover, the paneled surround of this wood-burning fireplace looked worn and dated and did not meet building code requirements. To make the fireplace appear as becoming as the remainder of the Tudor-style home, the owners tore down the paneling and had a professional mason cover the original bricks with rough-hewn limestone.

If your fireplace needs a complete architectural overhaul, do a little homework to ensure that the new face meshes with the original design detailing of your home. Visit your local library and check out books on period architecture; then choose a design that either recollects the past or bridges the past with the future direction of your home design. (In this example the keystone arch added to the fireplace facade mimics one found on the exterior of the home.) If you plan to add a lot of natural stone you may need to add extra support to the floor joists.

Once you've settled on a style and materials, sketch your final design out in detail, on paper or with the help of a computer design program. One way to visualize your design is to make a full-size cardboard model and then put it in place to see how your vision actually fits in the room. It is much cheaper to revise a design in cardboard than in stone! Have an architect or designer review your ideas; they may be able to update the design in ways you never considered. Have more than one mason bid on the job; be sure to ask for references and to see the mason's existing work. You're looking for a craftsperson who takes pride in attention to detail.

OPPOSITE: While it looks massive, this limestone fireplace is only 5 feet tall and 5 feet wide, in keeping with the home's modest size.

BELOW: The owners retained much of the original fireplace structure, removing only the decorative tiles that surrounded the firebox.

Look for the simplest solution first. A fireplace makeover doesn't have to be complicated or expensive.

Paint and Molding

With only four steps, this soot-covered fireplace with a narrow mantel was transformed into a worthy focal point: Elbow grease removed years of dirt and grime, a coat of paint added color to the fresh surface, a new mantel made from decorative moldings topped off the work, and a new stone tile hearth defined the space at floor level.

Even if you're planning only a modest facelift like this for your fireplace, have it inspected by a chimney expert or building inspector to make sure the unit is in good working order. Here, a chimney expert rebuilt the firebox, cleaned the flue, and evaluated the entire fireplace system to ensure that the fireplace was in good working order before refacing it. A couple coats of white paint, which matched the room's trim, covered up years of smoke damage and dirt. A new slate tile hearth that matches new stone laid in the entry, kitchen, and other areas, brightens the floor in front of the fireplace.

The finishing touches blended new with old. A wider painted wooden mantel better fits the fireplace's scale. Contemporary sconces, purchased online and hung over the fireplace, give a nod to Craftsman style and draw additional attention to the refreshed focal point.

RIGHT: **An affordable fireplace facelift preserved the original crosslike brick pattern in the surround, a signature touch of the neighborhood's builder.**

The Early American look of an old-fashioned fireplace facade did not match the owners' desire for a sophisticated living room decor. To update the wood-burning unit, the owners tore out the old mantel and tile surround and had a new gas insert installed within the existing space. Next, they added a custom-made carved limestone surround with an integrated mantel and hearth. The stone surround weighs nearly 2,000 pounds, but because the home was built on a sturdy concrete slab, no additional flooring reinforcement was necessary.

Most fireplace shops can order a custom-made limestone hearth for you. You can also find many carved limestone mantels online. Because of a limestone surround's weight—most weigh 2,000 pounds or more—you will likely need to have your flooring joists reinforced, which can be costly. If you love the look of carved limestone but have a limited budget, consider a stone look-alike such as plaster or gypsum.

LEFT: **Adding classic style doesn't mean losing modern amenities: A hinged glass door provides easy access to the flames.**

Hearth Accessories

Andirons

Andirons, sometimes called firedogs, are paired metal supports used to keep firewood off the hearth floor so that air can circulate beneath the fire, creating a more efficient burn. Viewed from the side, andirons are L-shape, with the lower portion supported by short legs. Seen from the front, the vertical members are highly decorative and serve to keep logs from rolling forward into the living area. More than a century ago, when hearths were used for cooking, andirons were also used to support spits for roasting. New and antique andirons are available in a variety of styles to match interior decor. Custom andirons can also be made to complement your fireplace surround.

Fireplace Grates

Fireplace grates serve the same purpose as andirons: supporting firewood and allowing air circulation beneath the fire for burning efficiency. Grates are more functional than decorative, manufactured of ordinary steel or iron grids supported by four short legs. Grates are available in different widths and depths to accommodate different-size hearths. Some grates are heat exchangers made of hollow, tubular steel. With the assistance of a fan, room air is circulated through the tubes so that it heats as the fire burns. The warmed air is then blown back into the room.

Fire Screens

Made of fine steel mesh and designed to prevent flying sparks and embers from entering living areas, fireplace screens come in three types: Folding

OPPOSITE TOP: During warmer months, a basic steel fireplace grate holds a basket of firewood, preventing the firebox from looking dark and barren.

OPPOSITE BOTTOM: Wrought-iron andirons hold a load of white birch logs inside this firebox so that a fire can be lit at your desire.

LEFT: This freestanding metal firescreen lends an old-fashioned feel to this contemporary gas fireplace.

screens have three hinged panels and are placed in front of the fireplace opening. Standing screens are single-piece units and feature a metal frame supported by legs. These usually have decorative scrollwork that makes them attractive accessories when the fire is out. The third type, curtain screens are made of a flexible mesh that is installed in a slot along the top edge of the fireplace opening. The two panels of the screen meet in the middle and are opened and closed by means of a pull chain, much like window draperies. When buying a curtain screen, it should be sized to fit the width of the hearth with enough screen material to create softly undulating folds when the curtains are pulled shut.

Tools

Fireplace tools are sold as sets that include a long-handled brush, a shovel, and a poker. Each tool is about 28 inches long and features a fireproof metal shaft. Sets include a convenient stand that can be placed close to the hearth. Use the brush and shovel to

ABOVE: This folding firescreen holds a multitude of votive cups that can light up the firebox even when the weather is warm.

RIGHT: This folding metal firescreen helps to prevent wayward sparks from landing on and singeing nearby upholstered furnishings.

clean ashes from the hearth floor only after the fire is completely out and the ashes are cold. The poker has a handle with a short prod and a backward-facing hook at the "business end" to manipulate and rearrange burning firewood. Sets are available in a black matte finish, or polished or antiqued brass.

Fireplace tongs use a scissors action to grip pieces of wood. They are invaluable for rearranging firewood while fires are burning, and for capturing and replacing logs that have fallen out of the burning pile. Made of heavy steel or iron, fireplace tongs are no doubt the most practical and indispensable of the various fire-tending tools.

Slings of sturdy canvas or polyester duck hold firewood to be carried from the woodpile to the fireplace. These rectangular pieces of fabric have handles at both ends and reinforced edge bindings. They fold easily for storage.

Basic fireplace tool sets on a convenient stand, like this set, are available in a variety of styles and can be purchased from home centers, fireplace shops, catalog retailers, and online.

Glass Doors

The latest advances in glass-fronted gas fireplaces include "invisible" glass fronts. Attached to a clean face frame with very little exposed metal, the glare-free glass is difficult to detect without touching it. Decorative glass doors, however, are still quite popular, particularly on wood-burning models, as they increase fireplace efficiency by preventing heat from going up the chimney when the damper is open and the fire is out. They're a handy safety measure, allowing you to leave a fire unattended for a moment or two.

Standard glass doors come in arched and rectangular styles. Depending on the size and shape of your fireplace opening, you may need custom-fit doors. Take your exact measurements along when you're shopping, adding a sketch if the opening is anything other than a rectangle. Clear glass allows the truest view of the fire, but if your concern is hiding the firebox when it's not in use, tinted and mirrored glass are also available. Polished or antiqued brass frames and hardware are most common, but to complement the other fixtures in your home you may want to consider nickel, chrome, copper, or basic black steel. If built-in cabinetry surrounds the fireplace, match the material of the glass frame to the door and drawer hardware.

Mantel Design 101

To add a little variety and enhance the visual interest of your mantel, start expanding on the basics and using your own sense of style to create a one-of-a-kind mantel style. Use your imagination—and all the tricks in the book: color, height, texture—and mix up the basics to express your personal style. Mantel design is a bit like jazz: It flows from a basic theme. Once you've composed your design, step back and see how well your composition works in the room. After all, your riff on the mantel has a whole room to play to! Here are some examples to help stir your creative vibe:

• **Symmetrical Without Mirroring.** Balance doesn't necessarily mean mirror image on each side, but it does mean matching in volume and weight. *At right*, the visual volume of the two candlesticks on the right is approximately the same as the plant on the left. Since the elements in the room flanking the fireplace don't match, this non-matching symmetry is a good choice. When the room's key elements are perfectly symmetrical, *lower right*, this slight imbalance is the interest in the arrangement.

• **Asymmetrical that Leans to the Right.** Have you ever noticed that many "balanced" settings tend to lean to the right? Look through this book and you'll also find perfectly symmetrical arrangements where the room's designer felt the need to add just one more item on the right. On the next page, *top*, the right-side emphasis is celebrated: It works particularly well because of the large mass of cabinet doors to the left of the fireplace. So the tall picture with a footprint half the width of the mantel actually balances the whole setting.

• **Repetition Even Steven.** On the next page, *bottom*, three groups of three items each create a playful mantel setting. The simple white mantel and surround perfectly anchor the whimsical garden setting. Repetition works well when it's clearly intentional, like this.

• **Repetition Tone on Tone.** Three simple plates, *right*, might be lost in another setting, but on this all-white hearth in a room that's colorful, the effect is serene and focusing. In this case, it's the "negative space," a lack of elements, that draws your attention, and acquiesces color to the rest of the room. A fully loaded mantel could overwhelm the space.

- **Repetition on a Theme.** Repetition is harder than it looks. A bunch of the same objects on a mantel may be boring. One way to add interest is to use the mantel space for a collection of similar items you love. In the image *below* (and on the cover of this book), white pottery collected over the course of time naturally has variations, so the items converse and banter with their different heights, sizes, shades, and shapes—but all within a range.

- **Repetition with One Big Thing.** When you've got the perfect art piece to display but the mantel seems bare, choose simple items that don't detract. At *left*, the art piece has a gossamer quality, and lightweight glass vases and white flowers draw attention to the art.

- **The Upside-Down T.** If you've got a tall wall to fill, the upside-down T is a good solution. A large element or grouping, *right*, marches up the wall to keep the hearth from looking bare. Along the mantel a horizontal line of items keeps the focus at eye level.

- **The One Big Thing.** Especially with a mantel-less fireplace, a one-big-thing composition fills the need to dress up the fireplace. Choose an item that is bold, *opposite, lower left*.

Two to Get Ready

To get started on mantel design, keep in mind two basic approaches. Mantel designs are based on balance, a sense that what fills up the right side has the same visual weight as what fills up the left side. But, like any rule, there are exceptions that work splendidly well. And, back to the jazz analogy, you'll best be able to vary designs when you understand the basics.

• **Symmetrical.** This evenhanded approach to arranging objects is universally popular for a good reason: It creates a restful impression of order and harmony. To achieve this classic look, center a painting or mirror above the fireplace, and flank it with identical size objects, such as candlesticks, ginger jars, vases, or statuary. At *upper right*, the objects flanking the center are identical, but another options is two same-size-but-unmatching items.

• **Asymmetrical.** A gathering of different-size items not centered on the mantel forms a pleasing arrangement. Asymmetry uses careful placement to visually balance elements of different shapes, sizes, and weights, *right*.

Chapter 5

Fireplace Know-How

Proper installation and periodic maintenance ensures that your fireplace will run safely and efficiently for decades. Because wood-burning fireplaces require a chimney and flue and must meet strict building code requirements, we recommend seeking professional help when installing these units. Prefabricated direct-vent gas fireplaces, on the other hand, are relatively straightforward to install because they require little structural alteration. For installation guidelines on prefabricated direct-vent gas fireplaces, turn the page.

Installation and Maintenance

Installing a Direct-Vent Gas Fireplace
Prefabricated gas fireplaces can be vented through a conventional chimney or directly through an exterior wall. If you are retrofitting a wood-burning fireplace with a gas appliance you'll need to have the chimney flue relined (and possibly resized) with an aluminum or stainless-steel flue since gas fireplaces can reach very high temperatures. Where natural gas is not readily available, propane may be an option.

Ventless fireplaces do not require any structural alterations but are not approved for use everywhere. For more information about ventless fireplaces, turn to page 103.

This corner-fit direct-vent gas fireplace, *right*, uses only a short section of pipe run through an exterior wall to send exhaust fumes out and take fresh air in. Because this type of hearth product draws in air from the outside, rather than from the room, it's a more efficient heater than a conventional wood-burning masonry fireplace.

RIGHT: **Relatively lightweight, a direct-vent gas fireplace is a good choice for a second level bedroom, sitting area, or office.**

OPPOSITE: Photo A **Direct-vent gas fireplaces can be readily installed on any exterior wall that is not overly filled with plumbing lines or electrical circuits. The units do require a connection to a gas line and a connection to an electrical circuit to support the blower. Have a professional install the gas line and electrical connection before starting the installation process.** Photo B **Existing corner windows were removed and covered over with plywood to make room for a mantel and art niche.** Photo C **The unit is framed in place.** Photo D **Drywall is attached to the framing lumber, then joints are mudded and sanded smooth. A coat of fresh paint completes the installation.**

Wood Fires

Building and Maintaining Wood Fires

One of the best ways to keep a wood-burning fireplace operating at peak efficiency and safety is to build and maintain proper fires. The type of fire you create, the temperature at which it burns, and the kind of wood you choose all affect the quantity and quality of fireplace emissions. Properly constructed fires burn cleanly and are less likely to produce creosote, a flammable tarlike substance that can build up inside flue walls and ignite into a roaring chimney fire. Properly tended fires provide more heat, produce less creosote, and leave fewer ashes, reducing cleanup chores.

Choosing and Storing Firewood

Different kinds of wood have different burning and heating qualities. The density of wood varies among species and affects the quality of the burn. See the firewood chart on page 161.

• **Hard or dense woods** produce an intense heat, burn for longer periods of time, and leave little ash. Because dense woods are a more efficient fuel and are also used extensively by the building industry, they have the highest price per cord.

• **Medium-density woods** strike a balance between heating efficiency and cost, and are a good choice for fireplaces.

• **Low-density woods** start readily and burn fast, but they burn at lower temperatures than dense woods—a factor that allows creosote to build up on flue walls.

All woods produce additional creosote when they are not completely dry or "seasoned." For this reason, buy wood in the spring and store it over the summer so that it dries out completely.

Store wood away from your house. Woodpiles attract ants, termites, and other insects, as well as mice, chipmunks, and squirrels. You don't want these pests to build nests in your siding or burrow inside of your house. Stack wood no more than two rows wide so that air circulates freely around all the pieces. Don't try to pack it too tightly—air gaps between the timbers help the wood dry. Purchase a metal firewood stand or build a platform to keep the wood off the ground which can also be a source of moisture.

During the cool months keep a small supply of wood indoors so you don't have to head outdoors for more

---

Fabricated Logs Firelogs are made of sawdust mixed with petroleum wax. They were invented in the 1960s as a way to recycle waste sawdust. Firelogs are often sold as individually wrapped logs and require no kindling or other starting material; they can be lit with a single match. Firelogs burn steadily and leave little ash. They're a convenient alternative to cordwood, especially for the homeowner who lights a fire only occasionally during the year. However, they are considerably more expensive than cordwood and aren't recommended for wood stoves.

RIGHT: **Building a roaring wood-burning fire similar to the one shown in this Rumford fireplace, is easy when you know how to pile the kindling and cordwood, as explained in *Fire-Building Basics* on page 161.**

Scrap Lumber Resist the temptation to use construction leftovers, such as plywood, fiberboard, or deck lumber, in your fireplace. The same is true for painted or stained wood. These materials contain toxic chemicals that release into the air when the wood is burned.

BELOW: To prevent logs from rolling and to keep air circulating below the fire, always stack logs on a fireplace grate or andirons.

WOOD SPECIES	DENSITY (lbs. per cubic foot)	Btus (per cord in millions)
Hickory	50.9	27.7
Apple	48.7	26.5
White Oak	47.2	25.7
Sugar Maple	44.2	24
Red Oak	44.2	24
Yellow Birch	43.4	23.6
White Ash	43.4	23.6
Cherry	36.7	20
Elm	35.9	19.5
Soft Maple	34.4	18.7
Douglas Fir	32.2	18.2
Norway Pine	31.4	17.1
Hemlock	29.2	15.9
Ponderosa Pine	28	15.2
Aspen	27	14.7
White Pine	26.3	14.3
Cottonwood	24.8	13.5
Basswood	24.8	13.5

fuel in order to keep the fire burning. There are several varieties of storage hoppers designed for inside use. Choose one that holds at least a dozen chunks of firewood at a time. If you have or are planning to add a built-in nook for storing firewood indoors, make sure that you use the stored wood periodically and restock it with fresh wood from the exterior pile. That way if your firewood is home to any wood-boring pests, they won't establish themselves in your house framing.

Wood Buying Tips

As previously noted, buy firewood in the spring to give it a chance to dry out or "season" thoroughly before the cold-weather fireplace season.

Firewood is sold by the cord—128 cubic feet of neatly stacked wood. The standard cord is a pile of wood 4 feet wide, 4 feet high, and 8 feet long. Insist on measuring the amount of wood you are about to purchase. Multiply the three dimensions to make sure you are buying a full cord. Don't buy wood that is described as a *rack*, *face cord*, or *truckload*. These are undefined terms and their use for advertising purposes is even prohibited in some states.

Buy wood split to no larger than 4–6 inches in diameter. The wood seller should have done most of the splitting work for you and included the labor cost in the price of the cord. Also, make sure the price of the cord includes stacking the wood where you want it, not just dumped at the end of your driveway. In many states, firewood vendors are required to provide an invoice that shows the seller's name, address, contact phone numbers, and the total price of the wood purchased.

Fire-Building Basics

Before you put match to log, make sure the damper is open and the firebox is free of old ashes. Leftover ashes may impede airflow and reduce a fire's ability to burn efficiently. With the grate centered in the firebox, crumple two or three sheets of newspaper and stuff them under the grate. Place pencil-diameter kindling over the newspaper, but on top of the grate. Crisscross the kindling to create air spaces all around the fuel—packed kindling will not burn properly. Over the kindling, place 1- to 2-inch diameter pieces of wood, again in a crisscross pattern. You'll want to get this stack of wood going before adding larger chunks of firewood—placing bigger pieces in now may disrupt your carefully constructed pile.

With the damper open, place your hand near the throat of the flue and check for air movement. Downward movement or no movement at all usually means the flue is cold and needs to be warmed. Twist two or three sheets of newspaper into a cone. Using the narrow end as a handle, light the larger end and hold it near the throat of the flue. The resulting updraft should pull smoke and flame up the flue. Be careful handling the lit newspaper. When the cone has burned halfway down, use it to ignite the newspapers under the grate. Once all the wood has started to burn with a vigorous flame, add large pieces, again placing them in a crisscross pattern to facilitate airflow.

Once the fire is going well, add cordwood, two or three pieces at a time. Keep the fire burning vigorously. If the fire is allowed to die down to coals and smolder for long periods, it may burn at temperatures cool enough to allow creosote to form inside the flue walls. The only time you should allow a fire to smolder is when you are nearly finished with the burn. Protect nearby surfaces from flying sparks and embers with a firescreen as shown on pages 146–147.

Never pour water on your fire to extinguish it—the extreme change in temperature may crack the firebox. Instead, allow the fire to die out naturally. Until it is completely out, don't close the damper. If you must leave a blazing fire suddenly, smother it with baking soda, sand, or kitty litter. Never leave a fire unattended.

Inspecting Your Fireplace

Fireplaces should be inspected annually. Potential hazards such as chimney fires can be avoided with an annual inspection, conscientious fireplace upkeep, and an understanding of the best ways to build and maintain fires in the hearth.

As wood burns, it produces water vapor, gases, and unburned particles. In a chimney that is clean and free of obstructions, these by-products are quickly vented through the flue to the outdoors. However, as warm air vapors reach the upper parts of the chimney they may encounter colder air and condense, forming creosote, a black or brown residue that clings to the interior surfaces of the flue liner. This is especially true if fires are not burning at high enough temperatures—for example if the fire is allowed to smolder and smoke, if wet wood is used, or if wood with an inherently low burning temperature, such as pine, is used regularly.

Creosote is a highly flammable substance that comes in many forms. It can be hard, glassy, tarlike, and sticky, or dry and flaky. If creosote is allowed to build up, it may catch fire. Flue liners for residential use must be certified by Underwriters Laboratories, an indepen-

ABOVE: **Use a powerful flashlight to inspect the firebox for any cracks or blemishes. With the damper open, look up into the throat to check for creosote buildup or cracks in this area. Before cleaning the inside of the flue, head to the roof *only* if it is not too steep and you have a safety ladder, and remove the chimney cap and inspect it; remove any leaves or other debris that may have collected on the cap.**

dent product testing and safety agency, to withstand temperatures of 1,700 degrees Fahrenheit. However, a flue fire can reach 2,500 degrees Fahrenheit. These high temperatures can crack brick, stone, or clay flue liners, allowing heat to reach nearby wood framing and other combustible materials, such as insulation.

The best way to prevent flue fires is to make sure the flue is free of creosote. Inspect your chimney once a year. Late spring or early summer is a good time, when heating season is over. If you wait until fall, you may not have enough time to complete any necessary repairs before the heating season begins again.

Making an inspection yourself is not difficult, but prepare to get dirty. Wear old clothes—including a hat—and equip yourself with a dust mask or respirator and a pair of safety goggles. First, check the firebox for damage or cracks. In a masonry fireplace, also check for brick and mortar that is loose or missing. Defects in a firebox usually can be repaired with refractory cement—a tough, heat-proof sealant available from fireplace dealers. A damaged refractory liner in a prefabricated fireplace often can be replaced without having to replace the entire unit.

Open the damper completely. It should move freely and sit snugly against the throat. Use a powerful flashlight to look up into the throat to check the condition of the damper. The damper should be sound with no cracks, severe pitting, or rusted-out sections. Over the years, a metal damper often will deteriorate from the water vapor and corrosive gases produced by burning wood. Broken or corroded dampers should be replaced by a professional.

Look up inside the flue and check for broken or damaged brick or defects in the flue liner. Vertical cracking in the flue liner is a telltale sign of a previous flue fire. Any defects should be considered serious potential hazards. Consult a professional chimney sweep or masonry contractor who is familiar with fireplace repairs (see *Relining a Chimney, left*). Be prepared: Fixing or replacing a chimney liner is an expensive job.

Look for any obstructions such as branches, bird nests, or other debris that can restrict airflow. Finally, inspect for creosote deposits. If creosote has built up to a thickness greater than $1/8$ inch it should be removed.

If you can't see the entire flue from below, you'll have to get up on the roof and inspect the flue from the top of the chimney, something that can be quite dangerous, particularly if you have a steep roof. You may wish to hire a professional chimney sweep to do this and to clean the chimney.

If you do decide to perform this inspection yourself, don't climb up onto the roof unless your roof has a pitch of 6-in-12 or less, and unless you are completely confident in your abilities. Make a safety ladder by attaching ridge hooks to the end of a ladder section. Use it by hanging the hooks over the roof ridge so the ladder lays flat and secure against the roof surface. Roof hooks are available at hardware stores and home improvement centers.

Cleaning a Chimney

Cleaning a chimney is not beyond the abilities of any handy homeowner, but common sense should prevail. You'll likely have to do this job from up on the roof, so take every precaution against accidents. If you'd prefer to hire a professional, see *Hiring a Chimney Sweep* on page 165. Don't work on roofs with a

pitch greater than 6-in-12. Wear a respirator, safety goggles, gloves, and old clothes. Wear good quality, rubber-soled shoes for traction. Use a safety ladder as described in Inspecting Your Fireplace on page 162.

The safest and most effective way to clean a chimney is with a chimney brush. These are usually big, round or square brushes with stiff wire or polypropylene bristles. These brushes are available at fireplace retailers and home improvement centers. Generally the wire brushes cost more but are more effective and longer lasting than the plastic versions. Both brush types are attached to a long flexible rod made of fiberglass. The rods have threaded ends so that additional rods can be added as needed. Tall chimneys may require several rods to reach from top to bottom.

The first step in chimney cleaning is to place a drop cloth in front of the fireplace to catch soot and debris. Next, seal off the front of the fireplace opening with a sheet of plastic and some duct tape. If you must tape the plastic to painted surfaces, use painter's tape.

Then, you'll need to climb to the roof taking the chimney brush and added fiberglass lengths with you. Use a screwdriver to remove the chimney

ABOVE LEFT: **Clean the chimney interior with a quality chimney brush and enough lengths of handle to reach the entire length of flue.**

ABOVE RIGHT: **Use a brush to remove any remaining debris from the smoke shelf, which is located above the firebox.**

OPPOSITE: **With proper installation and maintenance, your fireplace will be a welcome amenity in your home for years.**

cap. Remove the cap and then begin using the chimney brush to clean the inside of the flue. Start with the original brush length, pushing it up and down the sides of the flue. Then screw another rod onto the brush assembly and scrub another portion. Keep working in this fashion until the entire length of the flue is scrubbed clean. When you're finished cleaning the chimney, screw the chimney cap back in place and return to the front of the firebox. Remove the plastic shield and clean the interior of the firebox and the smoke shelf with a heavy-duty shop vacuum. Use a scrub brush to remove any remaining debris.

Hiring a Chimney Sweep

If you prefer to leave the messy chore of inspecting and cleaning your fireplace to someone else, hire a professional chimney sweep. Rather than relying on your local phone book, ask friends and neighbors for a recommendation or check with your fireplace dealer. These retailers often keep a list of professionals with good credentials on hand.

Although the chimney sweep industry is not regulated or licensed by any government agency, many sweeps apply for certification by the Chimney Safety Institute of America (CSIA) or membership in the National Chimney Sweep Guild (NCSG). These organiza-

Removing Creosote from Glass Perform this chore only when the unit is completely cooled. Clean the outside of glass doors on fireplaces, inserts, or wood stoves using a nonabrasive household window cleaner. Fireplace and wood stove specialty stores carry cleaning products made specifically for removing soot or creosote buildup from the inside surfaces of glass doors.

tions promote professionalism in the industry by testing applicants and offering continuing education on ever-changing fireplace technology and safety. For more information and to find a certified chimney sweep in your area, call the CSIA at 800-536-0118, or visit the website at www.csia.org. Visit the NCSG at www.ncsg.org.

For $150 to $200, a sweep will give your fireplace and chimney a thorough cleaning and inspection. Some sweeps lower video cameras and lights into chimneys to provide a close look at walls and liner surfaces and to establish a visual record of the chimney's condition for the homeowner. Many sweeps are qualified to complete repairs or will recommend a professional masonry contractor to do the job.

Proper Chimney Sizing

All wood-burning fireplaces and stoves, as well as many gas units, require a chimney. The chimney is the escape route for by-products of fire: carbon dioxide, smoke, and water vapor, and in some cases carbon monoxide and nitrous oxide.

Not just any chimney will do for every fireplace or stove. All chimneys should be lined (chimneys more than 50 years old may not be), and sized for the type and dimensions of fireplace or stove in the house and for the distance to the outside. A liner of the wrong size or material can allow hot airborne soot, ash particles, and fumes to cool before they reach the chimney cap, causing them to fall back into the firebox and vent into your home, creating a potential health hazard.

A chimney should be sized in both diameter and length to match the fireplace or stove. This information is provided with new, prefabricated units, and a dealer can get the information for you if you're changing an existing unit. Here's a rundown on the basics to help you compare what you have to what you may need:

• **Wood-burning stoves, inserts, and prefabricated fireplaces** burn at high temperatures, around 1,700 degrees Fahrenheit, and require vertical flues able to withstand intense heat. A key word here is vertical; the chimney of any wood-burning appliance should exit the roof in as straight a line as possible with as few angles as possible.

• **Pellet stoves** burn cooler, requiring narrower flues that can be vented through a nearby wall.

• **Natural gas fireplaces and gas firelogs** generate a lot of water vapor. Keeping condensation to a minimum is key, and a flue lining of stainless steel or aluminum is necessary. If you plan to change the fuel source or the size or type of firebox, such as converting from wood to gas, hire a professional to evaluate whether the chimney is in good shape, and to ensure that the flue liner is the right size, material, and configuration for the new unit.

RIGHT: When you're updating an existing fireplace, be sure the new unit is properly sized to your situation. New technology means that a new fireplace is not always of the same size as older model you're replacing.

Safety and Insurance

Building a fire inside your home requires common sense about safety.

- **Always keep a fire extinguisher handy** for putting out small fires caused by errant sparks. Install a Class ABC fire extinguisher near the fireplace and make sure every member of your household knows its location and how to use it. Most fireplace stores have small, decorative fire extinguisher storage units that can be installed in easy-to-reach locations near the fireplace. Check the indicator on the extinguisher monthly to make sure the unit is fully charged. Never underestimate the hazard of an uncontained fire, no matter how small. Fighting a fire is secondary to alerting everyone inside the house to evacuate and calling the fire department.

- **Install and maintain smoke detectors** according to the manufacturer's instructions. Your home should have one in each main living area, in each hallway, and outside each bedroom door. Change batteries in battery-backup units and battery-operated units annually.

- **Burn only firewood or firelogs** in your fireplace—never things such as pine boughs, books, gift wrap, or scrap lumber. In addition to creating harmful gases, these materials can float out of your chimney and cause a roof fire on your home or a neighboring house.

- **Never leave a fire unattended.** If you must leave your house before the fire burns completely out, smother flames with baking soda, sand, or kitty litter. Close glass doors or make sure a spark-arresting firescreen is covering the fireplace opening.

When you decorate the mantel, never extend decorations below the top of the mantelpiece. If you choose to hang garlands or Christmas stockings from the mantel, don't light a fire during the holiday period.

Insurance Issues

For the most part, an existing fireplace in a home is covered by a homeowners' insurance policy. The exception may be freestanding fireplaces, such as a wood-burning stove. If you move into a home with a wood-burning stove or add one after you move in, an insurance representative may need to come to your home to inspect the unit. Your insurance company can also supply you with safety information about installing and using fireplaces and stoves.

Check your insurance policy for coverage regarding the chimney. Inspections and cleaning may be considered basic home maintenance and may not be covered.

Owner's Manual

When you purchase a fireplace or stove, be sure to read the owner's manual and keep it handy. Every model is a bit different, and you'd be wise to know the particulars for safe and efficient operation. If the manual is lost or misplaced, contact the manufacturer for a new copy.

Safety Seals

Every new fireplace or stove must have a Consumer Product Safety Commission (CPSC) label that gives you information about where to place the unit and how to use it. This label does not ensure that the unit has been tested for safety. Nationally recognized testing laboratories for wood-burning units are:

- Omni Environmental Services, Solid Fuel Testing Laboratory
- PFS Corporation
- Underwriters Laboratories, Inc.
- Underwriters Laboratories of Canada, Inc.
- Warnock Hersey International, Inc.

Hot Tip When wood is not properly seasoned, it has a tendency to pop and spark more, increasing the risk of flying sparks and embers. If this happens, do not add any more wood to the fire and protect the area in front of the fire with a firescreen or by closing glass doors. Note that not all glass doors can withstand the heat of a fully burning fire so consult your owner's manual before shutting your doors.

When buying a wood-burning unit, look for a seal from one of these sources to ensure that the unit meets minimum industry-accepted safety standards.

Governing Agencies
The standard bearer of installation requirements for solid-fuel burning devices—which includes wood-burning fireplaces and stoves—is the National Fire Protection Association (NFPA). Visit its website at www.nfpa.org. Nearly all manufacturers design their products to meet NFPA specifications. Ask the dealer about compliance with the NFPA before you buy a fireplace or stove and be sure the unit is installed to this standard.

The Environmental Protection Agency (EPA) also imposes strict requirements regarding energy efficiency and particle emissions. All wood stoves sold in this country require EPA certification, but wood-burning fireplaces in some municipalities do not have to meet these requirements. For more information, visit the EPA website at www.epa.gov.

When shopping for a new gas fireplace, be sure it is lab-certified by an organization that is accepted by your local codes, such as the American Gas Association (AGA). Again, be sure the unit is installed to this standard.

Glossary

Andirons – Metal supports that sit in the firebox to hold firewood off the floor so air can circulate beneath the fire. An andiron *right* has a horizontal metal bar with "feet" holding it up. At the front and back are upright metal bars to hold the firewood in place. Often the front upright bars that face the room are decorative.

Btu – The abbreviation for British thermal unit, the amount of heat needed to raise the temperature of a pound of water one degree Fahrenheit. Often the amount of heat a fireplace or other appliance generates is rated by Btu.

Chimney – The enclosure of the flue from the top of the firebox to the point where the flue ends and smoke and gases release. More commonly, however, the chimney refers to the portion on the outside of the house, either protruding from the roof or alongside the building and over the top of the roof.

Cord – A measurement of firewood. A cord of wood is 128 cubic feet: for example, 4-foot lengths of wood stacked 8 feet wide and 4 feet high. Wood piled in and/or sold by the cord is sometimes referred to as cordwood.

Creosote – The black or brown gooey, tar-like substance is a by-product of the wood-burning process. It deposits on the flue when the hot smoke and exhaust gases hit the cooler walls of the flue. Creosote is flammable, and its buildup is cause for concern. Keeping a fire burning at higher temperatures helps to prevent creosote buildup.

Direct-vent – A gas-fueled fireplace is a closed system that sends exhaust gases directly out of the house through a vent without a chimney. These highly efficient units don't require indoor air for combustion: Outdoor air enters through an inner sleeve on the same vent that exhausts air.

Draw – The airflow in a wood-burning fireplace that pulls smoke, heat, and air up the chimney and out of the house.

Fireback – A cast iron plate that lines the back of a wood-burning fireplace. Often decorative, these pieces protect the back of the firebox.

Fireboard – A decorative screen, often painted, placed in front of the firebox when the fireplace is not in use. A fireboard covers the "black hole" of an unused fireplace.

Firebox – The chamber in which the fire burns. Fireboxes are lined with noncombustible materials to contain the fire and are configured to direct the fumes up the chimney.

Firelog – An alternative fire source usually made of wood chips or shavings and wax that have been compressed into a cylindrical shape.

Firebrick – Refractory (heat resistant) brick that lines the firebox of modern fireplaces.

Flue – The shaft inside the chimney that runs from the top of the firebox to the top of the chimney. The diameter, shape, and height of the flue need to be properly sized to suit the size of the fireplace to ensure proper airflow (draw).

Gas logs – Made from ceramics, refractory material, or concrete and shaped to resemble a natural wood log, concealing the pipes and nozzles of a gas-burning fireplace. A gas log set gives a gas-burning fireplace the look of a wood-burning one.

Grate – Rather than two separate andirons to hold firewood off the hearth floor, a grate of welded iron is often used.

Hearth – Originally the word "hearth" referred to only the floor of the fireplace where the fire burns, and could include the area in front of the fire that's made of non-combustible material (a slate hearth, for example). Nowadays, however, the term is often used to refer to the entire fireplace.

Insert – Used to retrofit an existing fireplace, inserts fit inside an empty firebox to change the fuel source and improve efficiency.

Kindling – Small pieces of dried wood that burn faster than full-size logs. Kindling is placed beneath and around the larger logs and is lit first to help ignite the larger pieces of wood.

Kiva – Constructed of adobe, these beehive-shape fireplaces have shallow, angled walls that radiate heat outward.

Mantel – A shelf over the opening of a fireplace that is purely decorative in nature.

Masonry heater – Originally popular in Europe, masonry heaters are stone wrapped around a relatively small firebox. The heat from the fire is absorbed by the masonry and released gradually into the room providing even heat.

Pellet stove – A type of wood-burning stove that's designed to burn small pellets of compressed sawdust. The pellets drop into the firebox at a regular intervals to maintain even heat output from the stove.

Prefabricated fireplace – Fireplaces used to be constructed "from scratch"

on site. Nowadays, the firebox and its surrounding structure are built in a factory, prefabricated, and shipped to the installation site. These units are made more from metal than masonry, so they're much lighter and less expensive.

Raised hearth – Building the fireplace several inches off the floor, often with a ledge for seating, creates a whole new view. Raised hearths are often used in dining rooms or other areas where furniture is likely to block the view of a fireplace that sits at floor level.

Rumford – Named after 18th-century scientist Count Rumford, these fireplaces *below* are characterized by shallow fireboxes, rounded throats and sharply angled side walls. This configu-

ration radiates much of the fire's heat into the room while efficiently drawing smoke and gases up the flue.

Seasoned wood – For wood to burn efficiently and without creating creosote, it must be quite dry, and the drying process requires several months. For example, wood cut in the spring and allowed to dry over the summer, or a season, will be relatively dry for use the following fall or winter. Wood that has been allowed to dry for at least six months is preferred.

Vent-free – By sealing a gas-burning fireplace and creating a super-efficient firebox, a fireplace can burn safely without venting to the outdoors. These units do still produce exhaust gases, so some communities have restrictions about where vent-free fireplaces can be installed.

Zero-clearance – A prefab fireplace designed to be safely installed very close to wood wall studs and other combustible materials.

Resources

Fireplace Manufacturers

Austroflamm
c/o Austroflamm Handels GmbH
Austroflamm-Platz 1
A-4631 Krenglbach
Austria
+43-7249-46443-0
www.austroflamm.com
Austrian manufacturer of Euro-style wood and gas stoves.

Dimplex North America
1367 Industrial Rd.
Cambridge, Ontario, Canada N1R 7G8
800-668-6663
www.dimplex.com
Manufacturer of electric fireplaces and stoves for the ambiance of a fire with no venting.

Fire Designs
1101 Isaac Shelby Dr.
Shelbyville, KY 40065
800-661-4788
www.firedesigns.net
Manufacturer of outdoor gel-fuel patio fireplaces.

Fireplace Manufacturers Inc. (FMI)
2701 South Harbor Blvd.
Santa Ana, CA 92704
800-432-5212
www.fmifireplace.com
Manufacturer of wood-burning and gas-burning, vented and vent-free fireplaces.
FireOrb
300 North Elm St.
Prospect Heights, Il 60070
847-454-9198
Manufacturer of a round, suspended metal fireplace with a 360-degree rotation field.

Hearth and Home Technologies
20802 Kensington Blvd.
Lakeville, MN 55044
800-926-4356
www.hearthnhome.com
www.quadrafire.com
Maker of Quadrafire, Heat-N-Glow, and Heatilator fireplaces.

HearthStone Quality Home Heating Products
317 Stafford Ave.
Morrisville,VT 05661
800-827-8603
www.hearthstonestoves.com
Producer of handmade soapstone wood and gas stoves; each stove is signed by the craftsperson who made it.

Jøtul
400 Riverside St.
P.O. Box 1157
Portland, ME 04104

207-797-5912
www.jotulflame.com
Manufacturer of cast iron, wood- and gas-burning stoves, inserts, and fireplaces.

Kozy Heat
800-23-4904
www.kozyheat.com
Manufacturer of indoor and outdoor gas-burning fireplaces. Innovations include "bay window" fire doors for 360-degree viewing. Also offers a wood-burning unit that can be converted to gas.

Lennox Hearth Products
1387 Pacific Dr.
Burlington, WA 98233
360-757-9728
www.whitfield.com
Manufacturer of pellet and gas stoves and inserts. Brands include Whitfield pellet stoves and Lennox fireplaces and free-standing stoves.

Majestic Fireplaces
410 Admiral Blvd.
Mississauga, Ontario Canada L5T 2Ng
800-525-1989
www.majesticproducts.com
A division of CFM Specialty Home Products, manufacturer of a large selection of gas fireplaces, stove,s and inserts. Carries the patented Insta-Flame ceramic burner.

Malm
368 Yolanda Ave.
Santa Rosa, Ca 95404
800-535-8955
www.malmfireplaces.com
Manufacturer of gas-and wood-burning fireplaces and the FireFlame wood-burning fireplace-BBQ grill. Also custom designs fireplaces.

Pacific Energy
2975 Allenby Rd.
Duncan, British Columbia, Canada V9L 6V8
250-748-1184
www.pacificenergy.net
Manufacturer of wood and gas stoves and inserts.

Rais & Wittus, Inc.
40 Westchester Ave.
P.O. Box 120
Pound Ridge, NY 10576
914-764-5679
www.raiswittus.com
U.S. distributor of RAIS Euro-style gas-and wood-burning high-efficiency fireplaces and stoves.

Real Flame
c/o The Jensen Company
7800 Northwestern Ave.
Racine, WI 53406
800-654-1704
www.realflame.com

Manufacturer of gel fuels, gel-burning fireplaces units, and mantels and accessories.

Regency fireplace Products
2206A Lakeside Blvd.
edgewood, MD 1040
866-867-4328
www.regency-fire.com
Manufacturer of wood and gas fireplaces, stoves, and inserts.

Robert H. Peterson Company
14742 E. Proctor Ave.
City of Industry, CA 91746
www.rhpeterson.co
Manufacturer of gas logs.

RSF Woodburning Fireplaces
c/o Industrial Chimney Co.
400 JF Kennedy
St. Jerome, Quebec, Canada J7Y 4B7
450-565-6336
www.icc-rsf.com
Manufacturer specializing in high-tech, high-efficiency, cleaning-burning wood hearth products.

2 Burn, Inc.
11735 W. Dixon
West Allis, WI 53214
800-776-6966
www.sunsorproducts.com
Manufacturer of gel fuels and gel-fuel fireplaces, and ceramic logs.

Thelin Company, Inc.
12400 Loma Rica Dr.
Grass Valley, Ca 95945
800-949-5048
www.thelinco.com
Manufacturer of pellet and gas stoves with and old-time, pot-belly look.

Travis Industries, Inc.
4800 Harbour Pointe Blvd. S.W.
Mukilteo, WA 98275
800-654-1177
www.travisproducts.com
Manufacturer of Lopi rand wood, pellet, and gas stoves, and fireplace inserts; Fireplace Xtraordinair wood and gas fireplaces and inserts; and Avalon wood, pellet, and gas stoves and inserts.

Tulikivi U.S. Inc.
1 Penn Plaza, Ste. 3600
New York, NY 10119
www.tulikivi.com
Tulikivi is Finnish for firestone. The company makes wood-burning soapstone fireplaces that cleanly and efficiently absorb and radiate heat into the room.

Vermont Castings
410 Admiral Blvd.
Mississauga, Ontario, Canada L5T 2N6
800-525-1898
www.vermontcastings.com
A division of CFM Specialty Home Products, manufacturer of a large selec-

tion of gas fireplaces, stoves, and inserts. Carries the patented Insta-Flame ceramic burner.

Vesta. Fire, Inc.
P.O. box 307
Manhattan, IL 60552
815-423-5018
www.vestalfires.com
Manufacturer of a ventless alcohol-based gel fuel fireplaces and accessories.

Virtual Fireplaces
www.virtualproducts.com
Specialized high-definition digital monitor that fits into existing fireplace cavity or into new construction to provide the image and sound of a wood-burning fire. Kick-plate heater is available.

Wilkening Fireplace Co.
9608 State 371 N.W.
Walker, MN 56484
800-367-7976
www.hearth.com/wilkening/info.html
Manufacturer of high-efficiency wood-burning fireplaces featuring the Ultimate Sal Airlight door, including the Intens-A-Fyre, Ultra Great and Magna-Fyre.

Woodstock Soapstone Co., Inc.
66 Airpark Rd.
West Lebanon, NH 03784
800-866-4344
www.woodstocksoapstone.com
Handmade wood- and gas-burning stoves, including a catalytic wood stove with the even, radiant heat of soapstone.

Mantel & Surround Suppliers

A+ Woodworking
P.O. Box 116
Cleveland, SC 29635-0116
864-836-2918
www.custommantels.com
Manufacturer of custom mantels, shelves, and mantel ornaments.

Architectural Salvage Warehouse
53 Main St.
Burlington, VT 05401
802-658-5011
www.architecturalsalvagevt.com
Antiques warehouse carrying salvaged mantels.

Carolina Architectural Salvage
c/o Cogan's Antiques
110 s. Palmer St.
Ridgeway, SC 29130
803-337-3939
www.cogansantiques.com
Salvaged hearth items.

Carroll's Mantels
417 CR 3321
Troy, Al 36079
334-735-3217
www.carollmantels.com

Custom-built mantel manufacturer.

Collinswood Designs
1400 Duff Dr.
Fort Collins, CO 80524
970-482-3610
www.collinswooddesigns.com
Shelves, surrounds, related cabinetry, over-mantels. Factory-direct sales.

Design Stencils
2503 Silverside Rd.
Wilmington, DE 19810
800-822-7836
www.designer stencils.com
Complete stencils for creating a faux fireplace.

Distinctive Mantel Designs Inc.
555 Santa Fe Dr.
Denver, CO 80204
303-592-7474
www.distinctivemantels.com
Maker of wood and cast-stone mantels.

Elegance in Stone
www.eleganceinstone.com
Fireplace surrounds of granite, marble, and limestone.

Foster Mantel
800285 8551
www.mantels.net
Hand-crafted mantels, shelves, and mantel caps.

Grand Mantel, Inc.
5552 Woodbine Ct., STE 11
Williamsville, NY 14221
866-473-9663
www.grandmantel.com

Living Wood Industries
4325 Chippewa Ln.
Maple Plain, MN 55359
952-476-4081
www.livingwood.com
Mantel surrounds in a variety of styles sold in kits with complete installation instructions.

Mantels of Yesteryear
70 West Tennessee Ave.
McCaysville, GA 30555
888-292-2080
www.mantelsofyesteryear.com
Manufacturer or reproductin mantels inspired from styles that were popular from the late 1700s to early 1900s.
Old World Stoneworks
5400 Miller Ave.
Dallas, TX 75206
800-600-8336
www.oldstoneworks.com
Cast-stone mantels and surrounds.

Salvage One
1840 W. Hubbard
Chicago, IL 60622
312-733-0098

www.salvageone.com
Large architectural salvage warehouse that sells surrounds, mantels, and firebacks.

Associations

Chimney Safety Institute of America
2155 Commercial Dr.
Plainfield, IN 46168
800-536-0118
www.csia.org
Find CASIA-certified sweeps in your area.

Gas Appliance Manufacturers Association
2107 Wilson Blvd., Ste. 600
Arlington, VA 22201
703-525-7060
www.gamanet.org

Hearth Education Foundation
1601 N. Kent St., Ste. 1001
Arlington, VA 22209
703-524-8030
www.heartheducation.org
Use the website to find local HEF certified professionals.

Hearth Patio & Barbecue Association
1601 N. Kent St., Ste. 1001
Arlington, VA 22209
703-522-0086
www.hpba.org

Masonry Heater Association of North America
1252 Stock Farm Rd.
Randolf, VT 05060
802-728-5896
www.mha-net.org
Use the website to find a local certified heater mason.

National Chimney Sweep Guild
www.ncsg.org
Also see listing for chimney Safety Institute of America.

National Fire Protection Association
1 Batterymarch Park
Quincy, MA 02169-7471
800-344-3555
www.nfpa.org
This organization provides helpful consumer safety information.

Pellet Fuels Institute
1601 N. Kent St., Ste. 1001
Arlington, Va 22209
703-522-6778
www.pelletheat.org

Buckley Rumford Fireplaces
1035 Monroe St.
Port Townsend, WA 98368
360-385-9974
www.rumford.com

Index